Contents

Dedication and acknowledgements   viii

Introduction   ix

Under threes learning outside   ix
Why this book is important   ix
Chapter summaries   x
Inspiring practice   xi

1   The story behind the book   1

The setting   1
The project   6
Overcoming difficulties   7
Parents   8
Adult role   9
Reflection and evaluation as a means to change   9
How the children changed   10
Young children developing   11
Our story, our experience   12

2   Awaking for Nature   18

Summary   18
The natural world   19
Sensory experiences   19
Loving the natural world   21
Children's and adults' stories – theory into action   21
   From birds to ants, there is so much to discover!   21
   Look to the sky   22
   Look to the ground   29
   Joy in all weathers   32
   Green life, multiple colours   33
   Growing plants   36
Myths about under threes   38
   Young children need to be constantly entertained   38

3   Play in the natural world   39

Summary   39
Discovery and understanding   40
Becoming stronger   42
Working together   43
Children's and adults' stories – theory into action   44
   The bigger and heavier, the better   44

Play with the unexpected   46
Water and soil – the top two ingredients of natural play   49
Collecting minibeasts and plants   54
Myths about under threes   57
Young children cannot focus on one activity for a long time   57

4   Becoming safe through taking risks   58

Summary   58
Defining risk   58
Adults' perception of risk   59
Why risk is important   61
Children's and adults' stories – theory into action   63
To see the world from a higher level   63
The tree house   63
Going up and down the hill   65
There is always a first time   68
Out of the adult's sight   68
Using swords and guns   71
When the risk is not worth taking   73
Myths about under threes   74
Children are not capable of evaluating risk   74
Every time a child faces a problem the adult should immediately help   75

5   Companionship and shared experiences   76

Summary   76
Social development   77
A dynamic and enabling environment   78
Shared understanding   79
A sense of belonging and connectedness   81
Children's and adults' stories – theory into action   82
Building bridges   82
Who is responsible for the watering can?   84
Family and friends   86
Guess who is...   87
Adults as companions   89
Myths about under threes   93
Young children cannot focus on the same activity for a long period of time   93
Young children are not capable of playing with each other
    cooperatively because they will easily enter into conflicts   94

6   Adults thinking about children   95

Summary   96
An interview with Gi   96
Why did you start this project?   97
Points to note when embarking on such a project   99
Research evidence   99
Is there any theoretical framework that inspires and guides your action?   100
Points to note when considering the theories behind the practice   103
Research evidence   104

Taking the First Steps Outside

Under threes learning and developing
in the natural environment

Helen Bilton, Gabriela Bento and Gisela Dias

Routledge
Taylor & Francis Group

LONDON AND NEW YORK

First published 2017
by Routledge
2 Park Square, Milton Park, Abingdon, Oxon OX14 4RN

and by Routledge
711 Third Avenue, New York, NY 10017

Routledge is an imprint of the Taylor & Francis Group, an informa business

British Library Cataloguing in Publication Data
A catalogue record for this book is available from the British Library

Library of Congress Cataloging-in-Publication Data
Names: Bilton, Helen, author. | Bento, Gabriela, author. | Dias, Gisela, author.
Title: Taking the first steps outside : under threes learning and developing in the natural environment / Helen Bilton, Gabriela Bento and Gisela Dias.
Description: Abingdon, Oxon ; New York, NY : Routledge is an imprint of the Taylor & Francis Group, an Informa Business, [2017] | Includes bibliographical references and index.
Identifiers: LCCN 2016020428 | ISBN 978-1-138-91988-4 (hardback) | ISBN 978-1-138-91989-1 (pbk.) | ISBN 978-1-315-68755-1 (ebook)
Subjects: LCSH: Outdoor education. | Outdoor recreation for children. | Early childhood education. | Nature study.
Classification: LCC LB1047 .B534 2017 | DDC 371.3/84—dc23
LC record available at https://lccn.loc.gov/2016020428

ISBN: 978-1-138-91988-4 (hbk)
ISBN: 978-1-138-91989-1 (pbk)
ISBN: 978-1-315-68755-1 (ebk)

Typeset in Bembo
by FiSH Books Ltd, Enfield

Printed by Bell & Bain Ltd, Glasgow.

Taking the First Steps Outside

Can one be too young to play outside? This unique and compelling book charts the experiences of a group of under-three-year-olds as they explore their natural outdoor environment, followed by caring and attentive adults. It deconstructs the myths that underestimate under threes and celebrates the importance of connecting children with the natural world and the influence of positive relationships in this early stage of life.

Taking the First Steps Outside draws on all aspects of working outdoors, focusing on different stages of the project, main achievements and obstacles, implemented strategies and benefits for the development of young children. Features include:

- Stunning photographs of children exploring the outdoor environment, who are interested, thoughtful, persistent and successful
- Detailed descriptions of real events, illustrating how the outdoor space can be an educational context for under threes
- Insight into the role of the adult, as they observe and reflect upon children's learning
- Advice on choosing the right resources and facilities to create a good outdoor learning environment for the young child
- Advice about risky play and promoting challenging and positive opportunities in the natural environment
- Guidance on how to set up an outdoor project for children under three

Written to support all students, teachers, practitioners and managers working with under threes, this essential guide will help you to develop your knowledge, build confidence and gain the ability to co-explore outdoors with children.

Helen Bilton is Associate Professor of Education at the University of Reading, UK.

Gabriela Bento is an educational psychologist and PhD student at the University of Aveiro, Portugal.

Gisela Dias is an early childhood teacher with a great deal of experience in working with children under three in Portugal.

When you first started this project what were your main concerns?   105
    Points to note when considering your concerns about such a project   107
        Research evidence   107
How would you describe your relationship with the families? How did you
    enable the parents to be happy about their children exploring outdoors?   108
    Points to note when considering parents   112
        Research evidence   113
How do you deal with accidents? How do you manage risk?   113
    Points to note when considering safety outside   116
        Research evidence   116
How did you improve your work – day in, day out?   116
    Points to note when considering the adult's role   118
        Research evidence   118

7   Resources and facilities   120

Summary   120
Planning the outdoor space – key points   120
    Dynamics of the environment   120
    Sustainability   122
    Inclusion   123
    Participation   123
    Time   124
Resources for playing, exploration and discovery   125
Fixed structures as areas for socialisation and physical challenges   132
Storage, transport and comfort   132
The relationship between the indoor and outdoor environments   138
Other spaces and resources   142

Conclusion   145

Bibliography   147

Index   151

Dedication and acknowledgements

To the children in this book, our 'sóis' (suns), without whom this book would never have been possible. We hope that as you grow older and read this book you will feel that our words do justice to your experiences. We will always keep in our hearts the memories of your dazzling smiles, warm hugs and contagious laughs.

To the children's families, for believing and trusting in this project, sharing with us their most precious treasure.

To our families, for the opportunity to have a childhood filled with outdoor play moments that influence our perspectives towards the world. Thank you for your support and strength.

To the board of Centro Social Infantil de Aguada de Baixo, the early childhood centre where this project happened. A setting that continually works to become a place where children feel appreciated, respected and supported.

To other professionals, community members and friends, who encouraged us and contributed in different ways to enable us to achieve our goals.

Introduction

Under threes learning outside

This is a unique book in that it charts the exploits of children under three as they explore and experience the outdoor environment, alongside interested and caring adults. There are images and countless stories of one- and two-year-olds caring for the environment and each other, making close observations, overcoming fears and obstacles, being patient, and demonstrating perseverance and fortitude. The overriding impression when observing this group of young children is the sense of connectedness and gentleness towards others.

There has been a strong tradition of children over three years of age working in the nursery garden or kindergarten in educational settings. For example in England Margaret McMillan set up the first outdoor nursery school in Deptford, London, in 1914 with the predominant age in attendance being three to five.

There has not been such a tradition for under threes to play outside in educational settings. Alongside this there can be the belief that under-three-year-olds can be problematic – the terrible twos is a term used to described the point at which children can see what they wish to achieve but do not have the ability to perform many of the desired actions. From this can come extreme frustration, anger and upset. However, this book portrays a very different picture of one- and two-year-olds and dispels the myths about these children.

Why this book is important

Many more children, and from a very early age, across the globe are now spending their days in educational institutions. There is governmental interest in the progress of two-year-olds as they have come to appreciate that this age is a time when individual special needs whether sensory, physical or cognitive can be more easily identified. Children are spending less time outside than they used to and more time attached to electronic devices. Although there is help on working with these young children inside, there is little for working outside with them. This book changes that. This book shows how the natural outdoor environment is an all encompassing learning place. From a basic physiological perspective young children benefit from the air, the light, the freedom and the exercise afforded when working and playing outside. By virtue of being in the natural environment young children come to appreciate, understand and love it. The natural environment affords the opportunities to learn and practise those necessary dispositions for life, such as perseverance, overcoming adversity and fear, and supporting others. Finally one can harness the natural environment to develop children linguistically and cognitively as they experiment and explore. For example, when carrying and distributing water they learn about body balance, the distribution of weight, the basic physics of pivots, that water is a fluid and that water can be controlled. The beauty of the outside environment is that it is freely available and always there. So this book is important because it clearly shows how and what young children can learn outside.

Chapter summaries

This book comprises seven chapters and a bibliography. Each chapter is illustrated with beautiful images of children under three years of age exploring in the outdoors. Chapters 2 to 5 each begin with an examination of the research literature pertaining to the chapter and each includes real-life stories captured by the staff as they worked alongside the children. Chapters 1, 6 and 7 incorporate the research evidence throughout. The chapter summaries are laid out in more detail below:

Chapter 1 sets the scene for the book. It describes the Portuguese day care centre where the project took place. It discusses how the project to use the outdoors with the under threes came about, the difficulties the staff overcame to make the project a success, how the parents were encouraged to embrace their children playing outside, the role of the adult and the centrality of continuous reflection. It charts the ways in which the children developed and changed linked to child development theory.

Chapter 2 reports on the abundance of opportunities offered by the natural world for young children to explore. The importance of connecting children to the natural world is revealed, and creating the fundamental conditions for meaningful learning to occur. It signifies how the study and exploration of animals, the weather and plants can lead to multiple learning and understanding.

In Chapter 3 play and the natural world are considered. Acknowledging that play is an innate and valuable activity for the child, we discuss how natural elements such as soil, water and other materials can offer interesting stimulus for under threes. We show how this type of play can lead to an improvement in health, development of oral language, clear understanding of concepts and the development of skills.

Chapter 4 explores what we mean by risk, and looks at the research associated with this theme, sharing wonderful examples of young children approaching risky situations and overcoming them. These including climbing, rough and tumble play and playing away from adults. The positive aspects of risk are acknowledged – the possibility of discovering that one is adventurous, daring, brave, strong, confident and successful. The role of the adult and the dilemmas they could face are considered.

Chapter 5 explores the development of close relationships between young children and adults in the natural outdoor environment. Moments of sharing, cooperation and empathy are revealed, contradicting the assumption that young children are solitary players. From the simple to the more elaborated play activities, the experiences shared in this chapter indicate that children gain a greater knowledge about themselves and others, contributing to the development of strong emotional bonds among the whole group.

Chapter 6 follows the journey of one teacher from not knowing a great deal about the educational potential of the outdoors to fully understanding and loving working outside with our youngest children. It charts a number of the obstacles she faced and how she overcame these, for example helping parents to be fully supportive of their children playing outside, diminishing anxieties concerning safety and being able to make and learn from mistakes made. Bullet points summarising each interview question enable the reader to easily understand how they can organise and manage outdoor learning for young children. The chapter confirms that with knowledge, skills and patience one can create a highly effective outdoor teaching and learning space for children.

Chapter 7 is practical in content and considers the planning and organisation of the outdoor space. It discusses which types of materials and structures can respond to children's needs and interests, identifying possible strategies related to maintenance, storage and preservation of the play environment. It confirms that creating an outdoor space takes time as the children and adults get to know it well and that it is not necessary to spend a lot of money in the process. It highlights that the families and community are key partners in achieving the project goals.

Inspiring practice

Einstein said, 'We can't solve problems by using the same kind of thinking we used when we created them.' In other words, if you always do what you have always done, you will always get what you have always got. This book is offering a real change to the way we work with under-three-year-olds and the chance to explore with them the opportunities in abundance that are outside. Although the story and episodes recounted here are based in a rural district, the natural world is all around us. For some settings it may be more challenging than others, but this is no reason why the natural world cannot be explored by all. It is there for the taking, for example the weather is with us every day and even a built-up area will have animals to observe and wonder about. Change comes from within – one needs to be able to imagine possibilities, be aware that mistakes are a necessary part of any adventure and be willing to step into the unknown. This was the type of journey undertaken by the staff in this book. One- and two-year-olds can achieve much more than we often give them credit for and they can achieve all this in an outdoor environment. The children in this book were kind, supportive, interested, thoughtful and intrepid; conflicts did not occur because the adults made their ambitions possible and gave them the opportunities to shine.

This book celebrates under threes!

1 The story behind the book

The setting

Figure 1.0 Centro Social Infantil de Aguada de Baixo – the setting where this project took place (main entrance).

The experiences reported in this book took place in a Portuguese children's day care centre (Centro Social Infantil de Aguada de Baixo – CENSI), located in the central region of Portugal, in a small and rural village named Aguada de Baixo, near the city of Águeda (see Figures 1.1a–b).

The setting accepts children from nursery to preschool (between four months and six years old) and has an after school service, including children already attending school (from six to ten years old). The setting also functions as a community support service that aims to help families in vulnerable situations. With this service, professionals try to develop a sustained intervention, in order to prevent or overcome problems generated by social exclusion and economic deprivation. The main goal of this service is to help families and individuals to develop the skills needed to create better conditions in their lives. With this goal in mind, the community support service develops small training courses, delivers food to those who need it and helps with the distribution of social allowances. Finally, the setting runs a small organic farm. In addition to the production of vegetables

Figures 1.1a–b The environment that surrounds the setting (open fields, farmlands and family houses).

and other products, the farm also aims to promote social and professional integration and act as an environmental and food education centre. The organic farm can be used freely by the children that attend the setting and it can be visited by children from other schools.

The setting (CENSI) is a private institution, but it is financed by the Ministry of Solidarity, Employment and Social Security. The families pay according to their incomes and the adult–child ratio is determined by law, according to children's ages. The centre has eight rooms, one for each age group, with varied ratios of children to adults, for zero-to ten-year-old children (including the after school service) (see Table 1.1).

Additionally, the centre has a kitchen and a dining hall, where all the children and adults have lunch and morning/afternoon snacks. For administrative work there is a reserved area and two meeting rooms where the early childhood teachers get together, usually once a week. Also, there is a big hall, used for staff and parents' meetings or other special activities. For the community support service there is an office and a meeting room to receive families with needs. The setting is open from Monday to Friday, all year (except for one week in August). It opens at 7.30 a.m., when children start to arrive, and closes at 19.00 p.m. Some children spend long days in the setting's facilities (ten to eleven hours per day), since many parents work late and do not have other family members available to come and collect the children for them. From 7.30 to 9.00 a.m. children stay with an educational helper or with an early childhood teacher, waiting for the teacher of each group. Between 9.00 and 9.30 a.m. all the early childhood teachers are ready and the day officially starts. In Figures 1.2a–g indoor play activities are displayed, illustrating moments of free play, natural material exploration and interactions between children and adults.

The daily routine of children from zero to three years old and the pre-schoolers has a different pattern. The younger children have a small morning snack at around 9.30 a.m. and they have lunch at 11.30 a.m. From 12.30 to 15.00 p.m. all the children take a nap and when they wake up they have another snack (around 16.00 p.m.). In the babies' room times for sleeping and eating are more flexible, according to the babies' needs. The older children usually do not sleep during the day (only the three-year-olds sometimes do) and

Table 1.1 Number of children per group and adult–child ratio in Portugal, as stipulated by the Ministry of Solidarity, Employment and Social Security.

Number of groups in the setting	Ages	Number of children per group	Adult–child ratio
Two groups	Babies (from 4 months up to starting to walk)	Max. 10 per group	2 educational helpers 1 early childhood teacher (part-time)
One group	Toddlers	Max. 14 per group	1 early childhood teacher 1 educational helper
One group	Two years old	Max. 18 per group	1 early childhood teacher 1 educational helper
Three groups	Preschool groups (from 3 to 6 years old)	Max. 25 per group	1 early childhood teacher 1 educational helper
One group	After school service (from 6 to 10 years old)	Variable	1 or 2 educational helpers according to the number of children

Figures 1.2a–g Play experiences in the activity room.

they have lunch a bit later (around 12.30 p.m.). The after school service functions during the morning, before school starts (9.00 a.m.), at lunch time and at the end of the day (16.00/17.00 p.m.). Figures 1.3a–c show the feeding and sleeping routines for the under threes.

Parents are welcome in the setting and they are invited to participate in activities related to special occasions (e.g. Christmas, Father's and Mother's Days). Usually there are two or three parents' meetings in the year and there is a specific day in the week when parents can meet with the teacher if they want to. Most parents enjoy joining in with the daily life of the setting, but they usually do not stay long, after settling the children. Times of arrival and departure are often used to exchange information and ideas between families and professionals, creating a relationship between home and school. Families are also available to help with different types of initiatives, offering their knowledge and skills for the benefit of the children (e.g. improving the outdoor area, participating in a community parade, helping with an Easter sale).

Figures 1.3a–c Building a relationship with children through daily routines.

The children that attend the setting come from different social, cultural and economic backgrounds. Among the families that attend the centre, we can sometimes find issues related to unemployment, poverty, alcoholism and low levels of education. However, we also find parents with high levels of education, with jobs in schools, universities, business companies, among others. The population that attends the setting therefore is very diverse, which makes it a rich learning environment. In the region most people work in industry or in commerce. There are many ceramic, metallurgic and wine businesses in the area. Given the level of industry the centre receives children that live in other areas and attend the centre due to its proximity to the parents' workplace. On average, the centre caters for 130 children.

In Portugal we have a Mediterranean climate, which is reflected in many sunny days and moderate temperatures. In the region where the setting is located, during the summer the temperature can exceed 30°C and in the winter the average temperature is 10°C. The rain is more intense during the cold months, especially between November and March.

The project

The interest in the outdoor space began in 2011, when in-service training about good pedagogical practices inspired the professionals as to the educational potential of natural spaces. Recognising the growing divide between children and the outdoor spaces and assuming that play in the open air brings benefits for health, well-being, learning and global development, the implementation of a project focused on quality outdoor practices took place.

Nowadays, children spend a large part of their day in formal educational settings, doing structured activities, oriented by adults. Time for free play is reducing both inside and out and it is important to counteract this tendency, offering children opportunities to play outdoors, where they can face risks, solve problems, take initiative and develop physically and socially. In this process, children should be accompanied by attentive and responsive adults, concerned with their needs and interests (Howard 2010; Laevers 2003; Leggett & Ford 2014; Maynard, Waters & Clement 2013; Portugal 2011; Rose & Rogers 2012). Nurseries, preschools and schools have an obligation to guarantee the right to play, consecrated in article 31 of the Children's Rights Convention (United Nations Assembly 1989) by offering time and quality spaces for free activity, inside and outside.

Despite these assumptions, in Portugal early childhood education is still too centred on what happens inside the activities room, wrongly considering that the main purpose for outdoor play is to allow children to stretch their legs and expend their energy. According to the study conducted by Figueiredo (2015), in the educational settings analysed, the use of the outdoor space was rare and the period spent outside was very short. Children only went outside in warm and sunny weather and showed low levels of motor activity and involvement when they were there (Figueiredo 2015). This view is not exclusive to Portugal. Indeed, across the world there can be a perception that play (and particularly play outdoors) is little more than letting off steam, with no discernible use to a child's general progression (Pellegrini 2009; Wood 2013) or that for young children outdoor play is a copy of primary playtime, of large groups of children rushing around purposelessly (Bilton 2010).

However, the centre felt differently about the possible impact of working outside with young children and indeed that children would advance and develop positive attitudes, values, skills and knowledge. With these ideas in mind, the development of an educational approach focused on outdoor space was interpreted as a dimension that could positively differentiate the centre. The development of the project demanded a strong investment in training and support to facilitate a change in educational practices. Theoretical and practical support was seen as an important foundation to ensure the professionals felt secure, confident and comfortable in developing an outdoor teaching and learning environment. The journey made by the educational team, as they tried to change their practices, was characterised by moments of joy, enthusiasm and motivation, but also by periods of difficulty, fear and anxiety that caused setbacks and demanded the implementation of different strategies to overcome obstacles. It is important to talk about the difficulties faced by the team and the solutions that emerged, because sharing those experiences can be useful for other professionals, teams and settings that face similar challenges.

Overcoming difficulties

Assuming that, in the early years, routines involving hygiene, feeding and rest are an important aspect of children's life in day care, the need to manage schedules was one of the main obstacles identified by early childhood teachers in the process of promoting good outdoor experiences for children. The amount of time spent with the tasks related to going and leaving the outdoors (e.g. going to the toilet, putting on coats and boots, changing dirty or wet clothing), plus the need to guarantee that the period of time spent outside offered children and adults the possibility to engage in meaningful play and interactions, was often seen as a problem that justified not going out.

> In addition to the bad weather that we have at this time of the year [December], children's mobility is still reduced: I have 10 babies between 13 and 24 months and some of them still don't walk alone. We almost never go outside. The only period of time when the weather is warmer and the grass is dry, is after the children's nap. However, we have to give them a snack at 15h30 because after 16h parents start to arrive to pick them up. In the end, we almost don't have time to go outside.
>
> (Gi, class teacher)

The need to overcome this problem and to find solutions demanded an intense and continued process of reflection and evaluation between professionals. Through an approach of attempts and errors, each class group found strategies to organise the time available, managing with efficacy material and human resources. Splitting the group of children and taking only a small number out was one of the strategies adopted. In this way, the time spent putting on boots, coats, changing clothes, etc. was significantly reduced and it also became possible to promote moments of close interaction between the early childhood teacher and the child. Also, the logistics associated with going outside started to be planned and organised in advance. As the project grew, the routines started to be managed in a more flexible way, accepting the possibility of delays or changes in the schedule when that was important for the children. Another important strategy adopted related to the promotion of children's autonomy. Adults started to encourage the children to take an active role in preparing themselves to go outside and return, reducing the level of stress and pressure on the professionals. With time children became more practised in getting changed and they also started to help each other in this task. Taking advantage of the excitement and urge to play outside, adults were able to motivate the children to cooperate, thereby promoting important skills related to autonomy, self-regulation, body awareness and group collaboration.

Parents

The support and involvement of the parents was a concern for the educational team. The professionals were apprehensive about the families' reaction towards clothes getting dirty, the use of the outdoors when the weather was not warm, and the interpretation of the outdoors as a dangerous area, more likely to lead to accidents. All the fears regarding parents showed, in an implicit way, some of the doubts of the professionals themselves, who still did not feel secure about contesting the parents' opinion and defending the importance of outdoor play. From the beginning of the project, we knew that family involvement would be a determinant to accomplish our goals. It was essential to consider parents as important partners in the educational work developed outside. Before the project got going we spent a great deal of time explaining to the parents what the project was all about and what we were trying to achieve. We showed them how our decisions were based on theoretical knowledge about learning and development of children. Outdoor play was a frequent topic of discussion in parents' meetings or casual conversations, since it was important to continually explain the benefits of this approach, to reassure parents' doubts and fears. Parents want the best for their children and knowing that professionals have the same concerns and goals sets their minds at rest.

Many families are concerned about academic learning and preparation for school and tend to forget or devaluate the importance of play. From our experience we have come to realise that parents feel pressured to offer the best learning opportunities to their children, aiming to give them the tools needed to face a competitive world. However, it is often forgotten that the best learning opportunities do not necessarily involve structured or directed activities. Being able to play with the child on a regular basis, to talk to them about their interests, or to enjoy sharing daily situations, are good examples of opportunities for learning and quality interaction between children and parents. Having become more aware of the parents' viewpoint, professionals adopted an empathetic and understanding attitude towards families, without neglecting the need to work with them in order to make them realise the importance of promoting learning through play and meaningful experiences (inside or outside). In this process, appealing to the parents' own childhood was an important strategy to make them more aware of the importance of having a connection to the natural world. Most parents mentioned that the best memories they had about their own childhood were related to outdoor play and they easily recognised that their children were not allowed to have the same experiences. They felt glad that the setting was committed to offering the children those experiences, since they acknowledged how important it was for them as they grew up. Despite this, the need for reassurance was a constant; parents continued to have doubts, complaints or divergent opinions, but we could deal with them as we had such a close relationship.

Involving the parents from the beginning of the project facilitated the establishment of joint strategies to overcome some fears or difficulties regarding the logistics associated with outdoor play (e.g. clothes getting dirty, exposure to cold weather). It was suggested to the parents that they leave rubber boots and waterproof jackets for their child at the setting. In a very short period of time, all children had rubber boots and most of them had waterproof jackets and trousers. Parents were encouraged to help with improvements in the outdoor play area and they responded in a very positive way. At the weekend or at the end of a working day, some families went to the setting to help the professionals construct new structures or improve old ones. This collaboration made families more aware of the importance of outdoor play and also made them feel proud to be able to contribute to something that was going to be used by all the children (see Chapter 7 for some examples of structures constructed by the parents).

Adult role

In the development of the outdoor practices, educational professionals showed concerns regarding the role of adults. Contrary to what was happening inside, where the adults were comfortable with a more conventional dynamic, in the outdoors many doubts and insecurities arose about pedagogical action, as can be seen in the questions in Figure 1.4.

Through these questions, which exemplify the concerns of the professionals, we were able to realise that the development of practice in the outdoor was not just a way to promote children's learning, but also to enhance professional growth and improvement. Each professional had to find their own identity in the outdoors, realising that there are no exact recipes or single answers for the questions that arose. The educational action in the outdoors demands rigorous observation, reflection and evaluation of each situation and child, deciding what to do according to the information gathered. It was the questions that were generated throughout the project and our reflections and actions that allowed us to keep improving and developing over time. We return to this subject in Chapter 6.

- Should I leave the children to play freely and just oversee, or should I play with them, accompanying what they do?
- When and how should I interfere/participate in children's play?
- How can I identify children's interests and decide which ones I should explore?
- In risky play situations, how should I proceed? If an accident happens, how can I justify my actions/decisions?
- What type of materials should I make available outside?
- How should I deal with messy play if I do not like mud?
- How will the parents react to dirty clothes?
- How can I monitor children's learning outside?
- How can I reduce and deal with the stress of preparing children to go outside and return?

Figure 1.4 Questions raised when thinking about children using the outdoor environment every day.

Reflection and evaluation as a means to change

The process of developing an educational approach focused on outdoor play is difficult and takes time. Research shows that changing practices demands an attitude of reflection, evaluation and critical thinking that challenges professionals to get out of their comfort zone (Pramling-Samuelsson & Pramling 2011; Wood & Bennett 2000). In this process it is important to ensure the professionals feel heard, understood and valued in their knowledge and expertise, recognising that questioning beliefs, practices and behaviours is a difficult task, which can become easier if it is supported by a group/team. Equally it is important to assure staff that questioning beliefs is actually a good thing.

The project involved monthly team meetings, in which all early childhood teachers and some members of the board participated. In those meetings professionals discussed and evaluated the development of the project, considering the different goals established. The meetings were important moments to analyse themes related to the importance of free play, the validity of children's initiative, well-being and involvement, adult style and risky play. The team discussion of these theoretical topics made it possible to create a common understanding about them, linking theory to practice. As the project progressed early childhood teachers were also challenged to monitor children's activities in the outdoor area and their own intervention through video recording, photographs and written records. They developed specific activities related to the introduction of new objects or structures in the outdoors. The data collected was shared with the team members, in order to promote reflection and evaluation. Photographs, videos and written records were good sources of information that enabled one to identify positive aspects, areas needing improvement, opportunities for children's learning and possible strategies to implement. The development of continuous evaluation allowed the early childhood teachers to pay close attention to each child, recognising their interests and needs in a more authentic way.

The large number of photographs that were taken were used to share with parents the experiences lived outside, facilitating parents' understanding and acceptance of the project.

How the children changed

In the early stages of the project, the outdoors was described by the early childhood teachers as an area where children had the opportunity to run and jump freely, giving emphasis to gross motor play. Children's behaviour was reported as being very boisterous and agitated, as they almost always engaged in the same activities. When children started to go outside more frequently and for longer periods of time, the outdoors started to be seen with less hysteria by the children, as they progressively gained a sense of familiarity and belonging to the space, as it became a place they closely identified with (Agnew 2011; Tovey 2007). With adult support and through the enrichment of the space with different materials and structures, children's play became more complex, allowing them to explore several skills and development areas (e.g. creativity, problem solving, and cooperation).

Another important aspect related to children's behaviour was the significant reduction of conflicts between peers in the outdoor area. This phenomenon can be explained by factors such as space dimension, diversity of materials and the existence of more challenges and obstacles that also promoted cooperation and sharing between children. It can further be explained by the regularity with which children went outside. They became used to and knowledgeable about the environment and it became part of their identity, thereby going out was part of their lives not an event. The adult role was highly significant in changing behaviours, as it became obvious that children's involvement strongly depended on the enthusiasm, motivation and wellbeing that the adults felt and transmitted (Bilton & Crook 2016: Stephenson 2003). As the experiences outside increased, children's skills improved. They felt more confident in taking initiative, without having to constantly ask for adults' approval. They became more autonomous, facing challenges with motivation and excitement. They progressively learned how to use the structures and objects, without being exposed to unnecessary risks. The logistics of going out became easier as children were keen to be more independent (e.g. putting on their rubber boots, going to the bathroom), making it easier for the adults to manage daily routines.

Finally, the project instigated the professionals to change and reflect on practices, habits and beliefs, with the aim of improving educational action. In many situations professionals acted in a certain way only because they had always acted like that and it was the most secure and comfortable option. For example, dividing the group of children, in order to offer different and more suitable experiences to each child, was never an option to be considered until the project started. The group of children were seen as a whole and the early childhood teacher felt reluctant about splitting the group for specific moments of the day. Overcoming obstacles and limitations was achieved by multiple strategies, but the willingness to experiment and to learn from mistakes was paramount in making changes. We felt the work we did helped children on their journey to learn, develop and grow into responsible, caring, critical and attentive adults.

Young children developing

Having talked about how the project came about, it is now important to discuss the development of the young child. There can be a tendency to dismiss children per se and for adults to view them as not autonomous, without a voice and in need of being organised, managed and trained. This view is often more prevalent when thinking about children who are up to 36 months of age. Everyone knows about the terrible twos, a period of time when the child is two years old and when a monster seems to emerge, having wild tantrums at the drop of the hat followed by floods of tears. They can fling themselves backwards out of buggies, they can hold their breath and faint, they can cling onto a three-wheeler bike with their knees and no amount of pulling can break bike and child free. Adults can react strongly to these mood swings, often reprimanding and making children sit on the naughty step or have time out to consider their behaviour. However frustrating for adults, this time for the child is likewise frustrating, because much of their behaviour is wrapped up in being able to envision what they would like to do, alongside not having the necessary skills to achieve those desires at the present time.

But these young children are fascinating and emerging and we should always remember that what we do with them will impact them forever. The child psychiatrist and educator Daniel Siegel (2012) argues that 'Early experience shapes the regulation of synaptic growth and survival, the regulation of response to stress, and even the regulation of gene expression. Experience directly shapes regulation' (p. 22). He goes on further to argue that genes and experience are wrapped up in making the person and that 'genes do not act in isolation from experience' (Siegel 2012, p. 30). So children are born different, they have their own unique personality and gene set and this then interrelates with the environment. Finally, he argues:

> For the growing brain of a young child, the social world supplies the most important experiences influencing the expression and regulations of genes. This in turn determines how neurons connect to one another in creating the neuronal pathways that give rise to mental activity. The function of these pathways is determined by their structure; this alteration in genetic expression changes brain structure and shapes the developing mind. The functioning of the mind – derived from neural activity – in turn alters the physiological environment of the brain, and thus itself can produce changes in gene expression. These interdependent processes are all a part of the complex system of our mental lives.
>
> (Siegel 2012, pp. 32–33)

We felt it important to quote a longish passage from Siegel because it matters: people in children's lives are crucial and how they relate to them matters. As an example of what Siegel is saying, think of a child who is very shy. Being in social situations can cause anxiety, leading to stress hormones being secreted. These experiences will eventually heighten the brain's response to change or new situations. So the experiences children have shape them through what information enters the mind, but then that reshaped mind will respond accordingly to the next experience. For every child we meet it is necessary to try and get into that child's mind and brain. It is important and most parents seem to do this intuitively to 'tune into' the child. When we are in a social situation we are not simply listening, we are connecting with the other person. We can test this idea by thinking about a situation that might be quite tense, say an interview. One of the reasons people find interviews stressful is that the interviewers, unlike most social situations, give little away, listening but giving few non-verbal cues. This can be disconcerting and off putting. But this demonstrates how interacting with others is far more than simply listening to the words leaving the mouth.

This does not mean we should have some utopian view of children, or childhood. The job of educating children is very important requiring responses from adults that are based on quality research, pertaining to body and brain development. What it does mean is having an understanding of the processes that go to form a child. Again, we reference Siegel's work; he argues that three aspects come together to form the child – mind (regulation), brain (mechanism) and relationships (sharing), all being 'three aspects of one reality' (Siegel 2012, p. 7). In other words, the mind develops and the brain changes and the brain changes impact the mind and so on. So the person has relationships with others, which impact the person so they react and then respond and the mechanism by which this is controlled is the brain. What is pertinent within this discussion is the centrality it places on the people around the child.

This brief look at how a child develops makes it apparent that children are not empty vessels to be filled. They are also not stupid, or incapable. Komulainen (2007) argues that we need to try and understand and thereby value children's own perspectives of their lives. Children find it very hard to express their ideas and feelings through the spoken word, but this does not mean they do not have a view. Jones (2009) suggests that one view of children can be of a number of negative stereotypes, seen through adult eyes. For example, that children cannot make decisions, or have opinions. We need to remember that indeed the United Nations Convention on the Rights of the Child, Article 12, states the right of a child 'to express an opinion and to have that opinion taken into account, in any matter or procedure that affect that child, in accordance with his or her age and maturity' (United Nations Assembly 1989). We need to think rather than 'doing to' children, to in fact 'do with' or 'work alongside'. Thereby having a less negative view of children and firmly remembering that they have a voice, coupled with understanding the science of development, should arm us with a better ability to support children on their journey. It is with this attitude of mind that the project proceeded.

Our story, our experience

Long before materialising on paper, this book was born in our hearts. Working together in the development of the outdoor pedagogical project, as an early childhood teacher and as an educational psychologist, we quickly realised that we had common interests. Despite our different background training we shared a passion for the most wonderful and amazing stage of human life – the development of under threes. In the first years of life each day is followed by new victories, words and dazzling smiles, making us feel privileged to be a part of such an important phase of growth, filled with laughter, hugs, tears and love. Likewise, we are committed to our role as professionals, trying to understand how very young children interpret the world around them and how daily experiences can be transformed into rich developmental opportunities.

As a result of these synergies, we started to record the experiences lived by a group of 14 children aged between 15 and 36 months, amazed by the way they explored and enjoyed the outdoor area. We can characterise the group of children as having strong and interesting personalities, with a powerful exploratory impetus and curiosity towards the world, and with whom we created tight emotional bonds, supported by the sharing of love and fascination towards Nature.

By recognising that under threes are often underestimated in relation to their skills and knowledge, assuming that they are not prepared to face the challenges of the outdoors because they are too young, we were inspired to share with others our experiences, in order to demonstrate how outdoor experiences can be richer, meaningful and captivating for young children.

Taking the First Steps Outside aims to be a simple and unassuming book, serving the following purposes:

- demonstrate, through practical cases, how the outdoor space can be an educational context for under threes;
- explore the potential of outdoor spaces for the learning and development of children;
- analyse and record the reported experiences with reference to pedagogical principles and goals.

It should be noted that the experiences described can be interpreted in different ways according to the reader and depending on the reader's level of involvement in working outdoors with young child. The ideas in this book may simply affirm what you already know, re-ignite something that may have been lost, give confidence to try the ideas or persuade others to do so. Throughout the book, we considered that it was not relevant to distinguish the author that accompanied the children during the reported situations, so we chose to always use 'I' or 'we' when we refer to the adult's role.

The adventures described in the book took place in a garden that surrounds the building of the day care centre, where there are tree houses, tunnels, shelters, sandboxes, slides, a blackboard and a musical panel. Figures 1.5a–d show the garden and some of the main structures.

The children frequently played in an area of land of approximately 1000m², located to the rear of the setting. In this area there are wooden play structures, a greenhouse, a chicken coop and a mud area. This space is constantly changing due to children's actions and interests, but the main features are represented in Figures 1.6a–e.

The group also visited, several times, an organic farm (about 1 hectare) managed by the institution, which is about 300m from the setting. The farm has big open spaces, greenhouses, small wooden shelters, swings, a sandbox and a small lake. In Figures 1.7a–d some areas of the farm are presented, although the dimensions and the potential of the space is hardly captured in the photographs.

Each context offers different play opportunities and, by observing children in action, we tried to progressively improve the spaces in order to keep providing fresh, interesting, rich and challenging experiences for children (e.g. creating new structures, offering different materials).

We challenge the reader to travel in the skin of our protagonists (the children) and to recall those moments in childhood when playing outdoors, finding small animals and jumping in puddles seemed to be the most fulfilling experiences of our lives.

Figures 1.5a–d The garden and some of its main features.

Figures 1.6a–e A space organised to challenge children in different areas, constantly changing according to children's initiatives and interests.

Figures 1.7a–d The farm as a space to get close to Nature.

2 | Awaking for Nature

Figure 2.0 The beauty in simple things.

Summary

The opportunities afforded when working outside are sometimes overlooked. Nature gives us a set of infinite experiences that lead to new discoveries and learning. To hear the sound of birds, to feel the grass on our feet, to appreciate the colours of flowers, to eat fruit directly from the tree, to run in an open field and to feel the fresh drops of rain on our face, are meaningful experiences that generate feelings of pleasure, wonder and freedom, which contribute to the development of a strong relationship with the natural world. These experiences are to a large extent simply available, if only we take the opportunity to go and seek them out. In this chapter we aim to report on some of the events and encounters that show those moments of enchantment and fascination, documented through close observation of children's play in the natural world. Also, we want to show how those experiences are understood from an educational point of view, which allows us to read children's behaviour and create the best opportunities for development and learning.

The natural world

Curiosity and fascination towards the world are innate dimensions of childhood. Contact with Nature has multiple surprises; discovery and exploration opportunities emerge, bringing joy and excitement to children's play. When we get to adulthood, we do not necessarily remember the feelings associated with the discovery of things. We can find it difficult to understand how simple events, such as contemplating a flower or finding an ant can be lived as glorious moments, worthy of admiration (Tovey 2007). With adulthood natural events can become trivial and we tend to forget what it is like to experience these things for the first time. However, if one prompts a group of adults to remember their own childhood play, they will always talk about being out of doors and will be happy with these memories. They may not mention the awe and wonder of the moments but more the fun and the danger. But as teachers of young children we do need to remember the power of discovery and thereby offer opportunities to make this happen for children. For a child, each moment in the outdoor constitutes a learning opportunity, being influenced by the:

- number of times it occurs;
- feelings that emerge;
- support given by the adult.

In the words of Carson (2012, p. 43), in the first years of childhood it is important to awaken children's emotions – 'a sense of the beautiful, the excitement of the new and the unknown, a feeling of sympathy, pity, admiration and love', so that they can be eager to learn, without being filled with information that they cannot retain early in life. A sentiment echoed by McMillan, the founder of nursery education in England:

> The garden is the essential matter. Not the lessons, or the pictures or the talk. The lessons and talk are about things seen and done in the garden, just as the best of all the paintings in the picture galleries are shadows of the originals now available to children of the open air.
>
> (1930, p. 2)

Through the descriptions of true experiences, lived directly by the children, we aim to illustrate moments of amazement and wonder with Nature, which promote the development of children's curiosity and exploratory impetus (see Figures 2.1a–b). These two dimensions can be understood as one of the educational goals in day care. From zero to three it is important to:

- develop positive feelings towards the understanding of the world, people and objects;
- promote a questioning attitude;
- create opportunities for children to make choices and develop strategies to satisfy their interests.

(Portugal, Carvalho & Bento n.d.)

Sensory experiences

Under threes' learning occurs mainly through sensorial and motor exploration. As Wells (1987) so beautifully puts it, children are 'meaning makers' – they are constantly trying to make sense of the world around them through their senses and actions. Therefore, we

Figure 2.1a Matilde discovered resin in the tree.

Figure 2.1b Leonor was amazed by the shape and colour of a stone she found in the river stream. 'Looks like chocolate!' she said.

need to offer children experiences through which they can activate the whole body and all senses, as they attempt to make sense of and appreciate the world around them (Gallahue and Ozmun 2006). These types of experiences give children a set of implicit and sensorial knowledge that will sustain future learnings. In Figures 2.2a–b the pleasure of walking in bare feet and feeling fresh water on a hot summer's day represents those moments of full engagement with the world.

Figures 2.2a–b Enjoying Nature in all its forms.

Regular contact with the huge variety of the natural world also promotes moments of complicity, sharing and learning between children. As Tovey (2007) argues, in a world where everything seems instantaneous and automatic, it is important for children to understand the different rhythms of Nature – learning to wait for the snail to come out of its shell or the desire to jump in the puddles of mud formed by the winter rains.

Loving the natural world

When we observe children playing outside we are touched by the feelings of joy, wonder and excitement that they express. We dare to state that it is impossible to be indifferent to children's laughter and pondering expressions, as they are surprised daily by the natural world. The enthusiastic reactions when they see birds flying in the sky or the sense of freedom when they are allowed to feel the rain on their bodies demonstrates how crucial the first years are for the development of an attitude of affection and profound connection towards the natural world. Indeed, we may assume that sustainable development can only be accomplished if children's contact with Nature starts from the moment they are born. In doing so, they will develop a sense of belonging and familiarity, through which they can understand their responsibility to take care of and preserve the environment (Huggins & Wickett 2011; Tovey 2007).

It may be appropriate to just ponder on this thought. Wilson (1984) popularised the phrase 'biophilia' – describing the innate attraction and fascination that people have with the natural world and all that is in it. Just note people's obsession and pleasure with going to other places, such as coastlines and mountains; there clearly is an attraction. Consider what we gain from the natural world. For example, the mussel's ability to stick to rocks was analysed to produce water-resistant glue; the gecko with their sticky feet led to the design of internal bandages; the hair and down of the polar bear helped with the design of thermal insulators and so on.

Many people feel instinctively that the connection to Nature of green spaces brings health benefits, such as stress reduction and a sense of well-being. Mitchell and Popham (2008) suggest that exposure to the natural world can help recovery rates from illness, improve happiness, reduce anger, improve the power of concentration and lower blood pressure.

Assuming that any educational action in the outdoors has to begin by awakening children to the marvel of Nature, the decision to start this book with this theme seemed to us both pertinent and suitable. We hope that through our stories we can enable the reader to feel as much in love with the outdoors as we and the children did.

Children's and adults' stories – theory into action

From birds to ants, there is so much to discover!

Outside, children's attention is captured by the small creatures that fly in the skies or hide between stones and plants. In an age when almost everything is new and learning occurs mainly through the information gathered by the senses and movement, contact with different forms of life promotes enthusiasm, curiosity and fear, allowing children to learn by first-hand experience how the world is. They need interested adults to ensure they do notice and they do stop to look or feel.

Look to the sky

The excitement of Alice when she saw birds flying in the sky was one of the most enlightening examples of the wonder towards natural life. Being just two years old, she watched with delight the trajectory that the birds took in the air and expressed her enthusiasm through exclamations and laughter. One time, we sat down with Alice and the other children, in the shade of an olive tree, watching the swallows flying over a hayfield as they searched for seeds. The expectations were high and our eyes were focused on the horizon. When the flying of the swallows got closer to the ground, near where we were, the children laughed and showed their excitement and admiration by saying: 'wow!' (see Figure 2.3). In this situation the adult was available to share that moment of happiness and enchantment, respecting the feelings of the children and avoiding any disturbance of the moment with intrusive interventions, such as questioning about the animal. The adult was aware that the children needed to contemplate and enjoy the observation of the swallows.

Figure 2.3 Alice's expression of admiration as she saw the swallows in the hayfield.

The discovery of a bird nest, in a flourishing apple tree, was also an episode lived by the children with enthusiasm. While we played outside, we realised that blackbirds were in a great bustle, entering and leaving the verdant canopy of the apple tree. When we climbed the tree, we discovered that the motive for such hustle was the construction of a bird's nest, where we could already find three small eggs. The children gathered around the tree, eager to know what was happening. The discovery captivated the children, who listened with much attention to what we said:

> The birds made their home in the tree of our garden. They built a nest and put their eggs in it. Soon, baby birds will be born here! In order to make sure that everything goes well, we must respect this space. We cannot make a lot of noise here because the birds might get scared and leave.

Confronted by the novelty and unpredictability of that situation, the children both smiled and looked to each other shyly, trying to understand the feelings of their friends. The possibility of sharing our garden with the new inhabitants and following their growth captured the children's attention. We felt that the discovery of the nest created an atmosphere of secrecy and thrill that reinforced the complicity between children and adults.

Although we explained to the children that inspecting the nest often could endanger the baby birds, we decided to take advantage of the situation to promote meaningful learning. It was with great surprise, that on our second visit to the nest, we found that the three eggs had already hatched. When the children saw the newborns, they were truly excited; they laughed a lot, as they realised that the baby birds moved and opened their beaks when they felt the children come close.

In conversations and play moments, references to the birds started to occur very often. Both in day care and at home, the children talked about the baby birds and even warned the parents to avoid making noises near the tree where the nest was. This demonstrated the significant impact of the nest discovery in the children's life.

As time went on, we made a few more visits to the baby birds and we talked with the children about the process of growing. Suddenly, one day we saw the young birds leaving the nest. In the beginning their flight was clumsy but gradually it started to be more secure and natural. The children witnessed the takeoff of the birds with great curiosity and they clapped when the young birds gained full flying skills.

When the nest stopped being used, the children had the chance to handle 'the bird's house' (see Figure 2.4).

Figure 2.4 'Where are the baby birds?' asked the children when they saw the empty nest.

At this stage, the interest of Diogo was so intense that he observed the birds' construction from different perspectives. At only 27 months old, he observed the nest standing up, then on his knees, then with his head tilted to the right and left, always with extreme attention to the object. As Figure 2.5 shows, Diogo (the boy in the middle) was gathering different information about the situation in order to develop a better understanding about the bird's nest.

Figure 2.5 Children carefully observing the nest.

From another perspective, the interest in birds was explored with the children through the discovery of dead animals in the garden. Although this may sound a little morbid, the dead birds fascinated the children and they were eager to understand and find out more about what had happened. Several times we talked about the cycle of life, trying to explain death in very simple words to facilitate children's understanding. For them, dying was like being ill and it was difficult to describe that it was a permanent state and the birds were not going to fly again. Then we found a small bird in the garden that had recently died. Its body was still intact and we were able to transport it to a table outside to have a better look. It was a unique opportunity, as all the previous dead bird discoveries had signs of decomposition and the children were advised not to touch the animals because it could be a danger to their health. When we took the bird to the table several children gathered around and started to ask a lot of questions:

- *What happened to the little bird?*
- *Is it ill?*
- *Why are its eyes closed?*
- *What are the feathers for?*
- *Does the bird have a tongue?*

We tried to respond to the children in the best way possible, in order to satisfy their curiosity and thirst for learning. With the help of rubber gloves, tongs and small wooden spatulas I opened the wings, the beak and the tiny eyes of the bird, so children could better understand its anatomy. The children were speechless when they saw the bird's tongue, represented in Figure 2.6.

They were also able to explore the animal, showing empathic behaviour as they touched it gently and carefully (see Figure 2.7).

By coincidence, a few days before we had talked to the children about the problems of pollutants for small animals, since they tend to eat the garbage they find in the environment. With that conversation still fresh in their minds, two-year-old Valéria quickly

Figure 2.6 'The bird has a tongue!' Leonor exclaimed.

Figure 2.7 Feelings of challenge, curiosity and intrigue support learning and the development of a strong connection with Nature.

asked: 'What did the little bird eat? Has the bird eaten garbage?' The adults were surprised with her question, since she showed a strong attention to what we had talked about and was able to make the links to that experience. I explained to Valéria that we did not know what the bird had eaten but we could open its body to check its stomach if she wanted. She immediately expressed her desire to see inside the bird, so we started to carry out an autopsy! With a scalpel I slowly opened the body and talked through the process with the children. I explained the importance of the feathers to protect the body and to keep it warm and I started to show some of the organs. When I showed the heart to the group, Diogo was keen to see that it was not beating. I explained to him that the heart does not beat when we die and I challenged the children to listen to their own hearts with the help of a stethoscope. Afterwards, we explored the lungs and the bowels, talking about their specific functions. The group of children around the table (Valéria, Diogo, Leonor and Xavier) were completely focused, ignoring what was happening in other areas of the garden. A moment of great excitement and expectation emerged when the stomach appeared. As I opened it with extreme caution we were able to identify small pieces of corn and pebbles. The children were fascinated and astonished. They constantly repeated the information they heard, trying to assimilate so many new and interesting facts. Their facial expressions showed eyes wide open and jaws dropped, as they stared at the bird with surprise and wonder (see Figure 2.8 to better understand their expressions). The time and attention they spent exploring the bird, and their questions and constant comments showed how involved they were in a discovery that was truly meaningful for them.

Figure 2.8 Getting to know the bird inside out – the autopsy experience.

Moreover, children's interest about birds was transferred to butterflies and similar animals. While playing outdoors, Alice looked for butterflies gently, with delicate movements. Despite her young age (two years old), she already knew where she was more likely to find the butterflies in the garden and she warned the other children to avoid erratic movements, since they could scare the animals. However, when a butterfly did appear, Alice was not able to contain her joy and excitement, as she started to chase it and call for our attention.

As time passed by and Alice grew older, butterflies continued to fascinate her. One day, when Alice was almost three years old, we received an unexpected gift from a lady who knew the children's interest in the natural world. Inside a cardboard box with colourful flowers, we found two recently emerged butterflies that needed to be released into Nature. The lady had a butterfly garden in her house and she thought that it would be an interesting experience for the children. She was absolutely correct! The group of children, especially young Alice, was astonished with the possibility of seeing a butterfly at such close range (see Figure 2.9). We explained to them what was happening (the butterflies were growing and it was time to set them free so they could fly) and several questions and comments started to emerge:

- *How will they fly?*
- *Will you teach them?*
- *Where are they going?*
- *I can't see their mouth. They have one, don't they?*

Figure 2.9 Alice and her love of butterflies.

Also, we observed images of butterflies in a nature book that the children already knew from other situations and Alice quickly identified the figure that corresponded to the species of the butterfly we had. The children observed the images of the butterflies with a magnifying glass and we spent a great amount of time comparing the images in the book to the real butterflies (see Figure 2.10).

When we went outside to release the animals the children were curious to see what was going to happen. We were able to place a butterfly in a flower and the children asked to hold the stalk. We told them that the butterflies were very fragile animals, so they had to be careful. It was delightful to see how they understood the situation and adopted a cautious attitude, passing the flower gently to the next person to watch. Because we told them that butterflies like flowers some children had the initiative to pick more flowers to serve as a gift. When we finally set the butterfly on an attractive flower and waited for the flying moment, a sense of excitement was present. Adults and children were excited to witness the situation and when we least expected it the butterfly flew and disappeared into the air. Sounds of joy and celebration emerged spontaneously in the group, since we felt that it was a moment of simple beauty.

Figure 2.10 Enriching children's experience by observing pictures of butterflies in a book.

The experience of setting the two butterflies free intensified the interest of Alice and other children, so we decided to contact the lady who offered the butterflies and ask her to help us create our own butterfly house. With her knowledge and some research on the Internet we were able to create a good environment for butterflies, following the process of growth and metamorphosis. Without being worried about specific learning outcomes related to science or biology, our biggest concern was to make sure that it was an engaging and captivating experience for the children, integrating different senses, emotions and creating the desire to know more, to be curious and to be amazed by the natural environment.

Look to the ground

To be aware of Nature involves accepting and respecting all the living beings that exist in the outdoors. When children play in a natural setting they can often be surprised by the minibeasts that appear or that land on their bodies, causing a range of reactions and feelings. This was the case with Leandro, 21 months old, when he discovered an ant's trail while he was playing with soil. He was intrigued by the ants and as he followed their trail he realised that they were entering and leaving small holes in the ground. When he tried to put one of his fingers inside the hole he was surprised by an ant that climbed up his hand. Leandro's expression showed a mixture of fear and amazement. His eyes opened with wonder and his mouth drew an 'oh!' followed by a slight shiver that ended with a big smile. He looked to the adult in order to make sure that it was a safe situation and he felt supported when I expressed positive feelings related to his discovery – 'You have found an ant, how marvellous!' Finding the ant's trail and the holes in the ground was something that called the attention of other children and Leandro felt proud about being able to share that situation with his peers. As Figure 2.11 shows, the children admired the holes and talked to each other about the 'ant's home'.

Figure 2.11 Following the ant's trail and learning about Nature.

Leandro's initial fear regarding the ants was replaced by curiosity as the boy started to develop an intense interest in small animals. Despite always having a tiny bit of apprehension, he began to love to look for spiders, ants, ladybugs, worms, etc., staying incredibly absorbed in the activity. He reacted with great enthusiasm when he found a bug and took care of all animals with kindness and empathy. In Figure 2.12 Leandro is observing a small bug in a flower.

Figure 2.12 Growing to love the natural world.

The enchantment of children towards small creatures was also visible when Diogo (two years old) found a snail sliding in a cabbage leaf. Fearless, he grabbed the animal with his hand so he could watch him closely. Diogo's expression showed fixed eyes, wrinkled eyebrows and steady lips. He was absolutely disconnected from everything that was around him, focusing his entire attention on trying to understand that living being. Without letting the snail go, Diogo twisted his hand to look at the animal from different perspectives. In Figure 2.13 we can see the boy paying close attention to the animal.

As the snail retracted and emerged from the shell, and showed his limp and fleshy body, Diogo shared with the other children his curious discovery. A delightful moment of complicity between Diogo and Alice occurred, as they shared the enjoyment of that discovery and exchanged expressions of astonishment. It was incredible to see how they respected each other's space and developed a shared comprehension of that phenomenon, being both only two years old. Figures 2.14a–c show the interaction between the two children in a sequence of pictures.

Unexpectedly, as Diogo observed the bubbling of the mucus produced by the snail, he started to get it progressively closer to his mouth and in a risky move he decided to touch it gently with his tongue. With all the senses activated in this exploration, Diogo showed an expression of revulsion that made me burst into laughter! By the way he reacted when

Figure 2.13 The mystery of a snail in the hands of a two-year-old.

Figures 2.14a–c Learning experiences gain a new meaning when we can share them with our friends.

he touched the snail I did not need to ask if he had liked it! In Figures 2.15a–b it is possible to see the snail getting closer to Diogo's mouth and his expression afterwards. Children need to make such discoveries for themselves to ensure they become confident in their own ability to stay safe. When children discover and interact with small animals in the outdoors, as happened with Diogo and the snail, the learning potential associated with this moment is immeasurable.

Figures 2.15a–b Not every surprise is pleasant – learning about the world by trial and error.

Joy in all weathers

Knowing Nature involves appreciating the different climatic conditions. Recognising the importance of a rainy day and enjoying the warmness of the sun are significant dimensions that trigger unique sensations and feelings. We recount two incidents to illustrate this point.

One day when we were playing with the children in the farm the sun suddenly started to disappear, covered by dark clouds. As the sky announced a storm, we decided to take refuge in the wooden house. There, comfortable and secure, we explained to the children what was happening outside. Together we listened to the sound of thunder and we waited for the arrival of the rain. A loud clap of thunder turned off the light. The children looked immediately to us, trying to read in our expressions the meaning of that event. Because we wanted them to feel secure and calm, we faced the situation with tranquillity and a good mood. We explained to the children why we had no light and when the 'ping-ping' of the rain finally began we all listened to the sound of the water hitting the roof and the walls of the house. We called the children's attention to that melody and together we tried to imitate the sound of the water falling. Xavier approached the eaves of the shed and stretched his arm, so that he could get the drops of rain. He tried to drink the water that stayed in the palm of his hand and he looked, fascinated, to the sky. Figure 2.16 represents the joy of playing outside after the rain.

Figure 2.16 The drawing power of a muddy puddle after a rainy day.

In contrasting weather, during a sunny day, a two-year-old girl, Matilde, fully enjoyed an afternoon in the garden, where she laid down on the grass, snuggled with the warmth of the sunlight and appreciated the effect of the wind in the branches of the trees. Matilde was fully absorbed in the experience and was calm and relaxed.

Green life, multiple colours

For young children novelty, fascination and wonder can be present in the most simple and routine situations. In Nature we find multiple opportunities to develop significant and captivating experiences that constitute the basis for future learning. Enjoying the sound produced by stepping on dried leaves or falling asleep comforted by the sound of the wind and birds, are moments of close interaction with the natural world that must be valued and promoted.

The environmental changes related to the different seasons can bring new challenges and discoveries. In the spring, for example, the trees displayed a luxurious green and the apple tree of our garden gained a new splendour. The tree transformation instigated the desire to climb it, as was observed in the behaviour of young Valéria. At only 27 months old, the girl decided to use a small box to improvise a step to help her get her leg onto the lower branch and climb the tree (see Figure 2.17).

Figure 2.17 Children are capable of finding strategies to overcome obstacles and achieve their goals.

Having succeeded in her task, she was quickly followed by other children and this started to be one of the favourite activities of the two-year-olds. Climbing the tree captivated the children in different ways: Daniel liked the challenge and feeling of adventure linked to the height. Tomás loved to jump into my lap from a higher branch. Alice regularly asked for help with climbing and enjoyed watching the beauty of the sunlight piercing the foliage. In those moments, Alice had a contemplative and relaxed expression, smiling as she tried to catch the small fruits or as she watched the leaves falling to the ground. Figures 2.18a–c represent the different experiences that emerged from climbing the tree.

Figures 2.18a–c The outdoors is experienced differently by each child, according to their specific needs and interests.

Growing plants

We also highlight the importance of experiences that involve exploring the growth and harvesting of plants. On different occasions the children had the opportunity to sow, plant, harvest and eat what the land produces, learning many things in a spontaneous and natural way. On the days spent on the farm, on visits to home gardens or on walks within the community children were encouraged to pay attention and value the different signs of Nature.

On the farm, for example, the strawberry season was lived by the children with great enthusiasm since they loved to harvest and eat the small red fruits! With voracious appetites the children ate the strawberries as soon as they were picked and they were never satisfied (see Figures 2.19a–b)! We happily remember young Vicente (two years old) with his hands and knees on the ground, biting the strawberries without separating them from the plant. Valéria, of the same age, started to eat this fruit for the first time on the days spent on the farm, showing great pleasure, even though she rejected the fruit at home. When we told her mother that she had started to eat fruit, the mother reacted with admiration and joy. That small change was a sign that her daughter was growing up happy in day care and willing to partake in new experiences.

Figures 2.19a–b Outdoor play increases children's appetite.

Other adventures on the farm included Alice's satisfaction and persistence when eating tomatoes. With the red pulp sliding down her chin, she gripped the tomato vigorously, amused with the task. As it is possible to see in Figure 2.20a, sometimes the tomato was too big for her hands and mouth, but that did not stop her from eating it with pleasure.

Likewise, we were delighted to see children eating carrots that had been recently picked from the ground, as Daniel is in Figure 2.20b. The children were not aware that carrots grow like that and this discovery promoted a desire to taste. After eating the carrots in playful and spontaneous situations they also started to eat these vegetables in the setting and at home with fewer complaints.

When I took the children to visit my parents' garden or when we went to walk in the community it was incredible to see how they were eager to try everything, eating rough spinach, rocket and lettuce, among other things. For my parents and other villagers it was very important to see the children enjoying and showing interest in farm products. On the walks we could see that the children were very open to everything that was around

Figures 2.20a–b Promoting healthy eating habits from an early age. In the outdoors children appreciate fresh fruits and vegetables.

them, making several comments that showed their interest about Nature. They often called our attention to the smell and shape of plants or trees (e.g. 'Look at that plant, it looks like little pineapples!') and they displayed interest when we showed them how peas, wheat, lupines, among other things, were cultivated. Figures 2.21a–b show children smelling aromatic herbs that grew in the greenhouse of the farm.

Figures 2.21a–b 'This herb is like the tea my grandmother makes me when I'm ill!' said one of the children. Smells can remind us of different places and people.

The experience of discovering different types of food is significant in many ways. It allowed the children to try new flavours, textures and smells, gaining initial understanding of the process of growth. It allowed them to appreciate the wonders of the natural world through shared experiences with significant adults and friends.

We hope these examples of children experiencing and discovering the natural world have demonstrated how children make sense of it, how they build knowledge, understanding and appreciation of it and how this in turn brings them a love of it. The advantage of the natural world is that it is there, to be enjoyed and learnt from.

Myths about under threes

Young children need to be constantly entertained

Without devaluating the need and importance of stimulating under threes to help them develop skills and knowledge, it is important to reflect on the negative consequences of overstimulation. Children need time to process and integrate the great amount of information that they receive every day, so it is crucial to understand children's rhythm. They need time to experience and appreciate silence and calm thereby creating a balance between more exciting experiences. Often, due to the pressure felt by the adults to do or teach things, moments for serenity tend to be avoided with activities aimed at filling the empty spaces (e.g. sing a song, do a drawing). It is important to keep in mind that the adult does not need to adopt an entertainer role. Taking the time to carefully observe children is important and it does not mean that we are doing nothing or that we are neglecting our responsibility as an educator.

To support outdoor play and to awaken children to Nature it is fundamental to acknowledge the importance of silence and contemplation. Beauty in Nature can only be truly admired if we feel connected and available to receive the inputs from the environment, without being overwhelmed with too much information.

Promoting self-regulation during childhood is an important educational goal that contradicts that idea that young children need to be entertained. A self-regulated child is able to find interests and be self-motivated without needing constant external reinforcement.

3 Play in the natural world

Figure 3.0 Exploring sounds and rhythms through natural materials.

Summary

Play in natural environments allows you to explore a variety of elements that raise children's interest. Sticks, tree trunks, small twigs, rocks, soil, pine cones, leaves, moss, living beings, among others, enhance different activities, promoting curiosity and the exploratory impetus. Often, what Nature offers spontaneously and unpredictably is more interesting to children than manufactured plastic objects with a unique purpose. Natural elements are multisensory, enabling different discoveries based on the interests and characteristics of each child (Woolley & Lowe 2013).

According to investigations carried out on this subject area, natural spaces enhance play and facilitate the development of skills associated with creativity, physical activity, problem solving and teamwork (Fjørtoft 2004; Herrington & Studtmann 1998; Tranter & Malone 2004). The experiences around the exploration of natural elements allow the acquisition of information about the world, leading to the progressive construction of knowledge related to the environment and the effects of our actions in it. Figure 3.1 serves as an example of this in which children are discovering Nature by playing with cabbage leaves.

Figure 3.1 Simple experiences can promote rich learning opportunities.

Discovery and understanding

When children explore natural materials they are driven by curiosity and a drive to learn. Through actions, children discover different ways to use objects, giving them multiple functions and meanings. With imagination and creativity, sticks can be used as pistols/guns, recreating a film; like boats, floating in a pool of water; or as pencils, drawing marks in the sand (as the young girl in Figure 3.2 is doing). In this process of constant reinvention and assigning new meanings to the objects, it becomes possible to mobilise notions related to science, language and mathematics.

It thereby follows that the possibility of touching, experimenting and repeating stimulates different parts of the body and can be considered as a way to learn. It is important to bear in mind that repetition in children's actions does not necessarily mean lack of interest or reduce complexity in the task. Repetition can be understood as an important learning strategy, through which the child gains new information about a phenomenon, gradually internalising the processes underlying it and developing mental schemas (Athey 2007; Bilton 2010; Nutbrown 2011). While filling and emptying, several times, containers with soil or water, a child grasps, for example, concepts related to weight (e.g. when the bucket is full it is heavier), volume (e.g. it is necessary to dig out a lot of soil to fill

Figure 3.2 Natural materials are very easy to find and offer many benefits. With them children are inspired to think outside the box.

the bucket) and time (e.g. it is quicker to fill the bucket with water than with soil). In these situations, the child enjoys the process, without worrying about the outcome of the action. The sense of challenge and interest in a certain phenomenon is presented as a plausible justification for the behaviour and indeed a real motivation. This search for meaning and the patterns of certainty will also mean children are faced with dilemmas, where what the mind considers a pattern is being confounded by some new information. For example, a large box may feel very light in weight. This conundrum has to be solved and this will happen through repeated experimentation until the puzzle is solved and new information stored mentally. Often, the need to establish goals appears associated with adult intervention. Although well intended, adults tend to question children in an intrusive way, presenting an attitude of disregard towards free play. According to Tovey (2007, p. 142), '[y]oung children are often confused by a style of interaction where questions are not for puzzling and for finding out, but are used for testing'. Mercer (2008) argues for teachers to fully appreciate the link between talking and thinking and the importance of their role in facilitating opportunities for children to learn, understand and make sense through conversations. Further, it is argued that quality conversations that develop oracy and understanding involve:

- children asking questions;
- the talk being about current interests or happenings;
- conversations often being lengthy;
- the adult demonstrating genuine interest;
- learning occurring without direct teaching and not involving the interrogatory style question/answer dialogue.

(Mercer & Littleton 2007)

The wonderful thing about the discovery of natural elements is that it instigates questions and dialogues between children and adults. In these situations, language has a mediating role, giving meaning to what the child sees, thinks and feels (Tovey 2007). The possibility of naming a phenomenon or object is a central dimension to understanding the world and to developing a critical and curious attitude from an early age. Children need to have the language to be well equipped in the world (Goswami 2013).

Becoming stronger

Play with natural elements also involves risks, since it is difficult to anticipate or control what the child will find in the space. The theme of risky play will be developed in more detail in Chapter 4, but it is important to note that the possibility of accidents when playing with natural elements cannot be used as a justification to ban the use of these elements by children, since its benefits, as we have been emphasising, are very relevant. Risk is associated with a feeling of overcoming limits that promotes children's self-esteem and trust in their skills. The strength to carry a large stick or the skill to throw a heavy stone are examples of risky activities that captivate children by providing rich information about their bodies and their possibilities in relation to space. In Figure 3.3 the boy is stretching his body to prepare himself to deal with the risk of jumping from a higher level.

Figure 3.3 Knowing about how our body behaves and what it is capable of is crucial to face risky situations. Learning experiences that stimulate body and mind tend to be more meaningful and long-lasting.

Interaction with natural elements such as soil helps build immunity. Part of the natural flora of the soil is pathogenic. Contact with soil therefore brings health benefits. Early contact with such microorganisms helps ensures lifelong immunity, so in later life when people get cuts they very rarely go sceptic (Boschma 2013). Equally important is the possibility of getting our hands dirty, learning through the tactile experience to understand what such a material can and cannot do.

Working together

Finally, natural spaces can also be understood as important contexts for interactions between children. When they are confronted with unexpected challenges, children feel the need to cooperate, share ideas, strategies, fears and desires. With peers, overcoming obstacles generates satisfaction and motivation towards teamwork and learning occurs in a spontaneous way, as the roles of teacher and learner switch according to the tasks. Figures 3.4a–b represent a situation when the children helped each other to shell beans, a difficult task that requires accuracy in fine motor skills. In the outdoors children reveal skills that are hidden during the time spent inside, making it very important for the adult to pay attention to the children's play, gaining information to support learning and development (Maynard, Waters & Clement 2013).

Having in mind the theoretical ideas presented here, in this chapter we share some experiences related to the value of play in natural spaces. Interest in the natural elements grows as children become more agile and autonomous in the space outdoors, being able to develop their initiative to achieve their interests. It is impossible to describe all the moments we have experienced with the children so we will share a few examples to illustrate the breadth of possibilities available when working outside with young children.

Figures 3.4a–b Going beyond paper and pencil activities to promote fine motor skills.

Children's and adults' stories – theory into action

The bigger and heavier, the better

Walks around the community are good examples of experiences that allow for the exploration of natural elements. In the beginning of spring we went for a walk with the children, crossing through the village via a path that ran parallel to a small stream. As we walked next to the water, the children started to grab different materials and a group of boys who were two years old were very interested in collecting big sticks (Marcos, Tomás and Daniel). They searched for the sticks eagerly and when they found one, they carried the sticks along the path, showing feelings of pride and satisfaction. Sometimes they switched the sticks with another child or started to look for another one, hoping to find an even bigger and more challenging one. Carrying the stick developed skills of motor coordination, strengthened muscles and demonstrated their power and skill. It also had a dimension of risk, which made it even more interesting (see Figures 3.5a–b to understand children's excitement with the big sticks and their admiration when they found a tilted tree trunk in the woods).

Figures 3.5a–b The interest for the big and heavy can be expressed in different ways. Children can feel challenged and motivated to play with sticks and they can also admire the 'size' of Nature, represented by a tree trunk.

As we progressed the big sticks acquired different purposes. The boys used the sticks to play swords, laughing every time the 'weapons' touched. They also made use of them to play in the stream. Daniel was fascinated by the effect the stick produced in the water and he called my attention to it. Taking advantage of his interest, I suggested that he throw the stick into the water to see what would happen. The little boy was very surprised when he realised the stick travelled away with the flow, remaining at water surface. Inspired by this first experience, we decided to throw rocks of different sizes, observing and talking about the effects on the water caused by the different objects. After several attempts Daniel began to understand that, although it was easier to throw small rocks, the bigger ones produced a greater impact on the water (see Figure 3.6). The strong splashes instigated his curiosity and the will to continue. Outcomes and comparison of outcomes produced new knowledge for the child. This is a classic example of a schema in action, a repeatable behaviour enabling the child to make sense of the world.

Figure 3.6 Experimentation and repetition are learning strategies. Like scientists, children should have different opportunities to test hypotheses and develop theories about phenomena.

Through the experiences in the outdoors of the day care centre the interest for the big and heavy also became evident. Some children spent a lot of time searching, carrying and throwing heavy objects around. The logs that had been forgotten and did not appear to have any use, gained a new purpose as the children started to carry them from one place to another. To accomplish this task the children needed to work together. They evidently felt excited by the difficulty of manipulating the log, which clearly exceeded their height and weight. To carry the log, the children had to organise themselves, establishing group strategies to accomplish the desired goals (see Figure 3.7).

Figure 3.7 Outdoor play promotes cooperation among children.

For example, it was a truly challenging task to cross the entire garden with their arms tight around the log and put it between the tree branches so they could climb up it (Figures 3.8a–d represents the sequence of events). Although it took a while to achieve this and they had many trials and errors the children did not give up and were keen to be successful. They stumbled and fell several times, always getting up with laughter and motivation to keep the play going.

Figures 3.8a–d While playing with others the outcome is not as important as the shared joy and excitement during the process.

Play with the unexpected

As we have already illustrated in the last chapter, outdoor play also benefits from weather changes that create rich opportunities for play, promoting high levels of well-being and involvement.

In this context, consider our surprise (children and adults) when we found an extensive carpet of mushrooms that grew in the field after many days of rain. The children closely observed the strange velvety surface and quickly realised that not all the mushrooms were the same. They were different sizes, colours and shapes and each produced a specific smell. To ensure children's safety, we talked about the danger of putting the mushrooms in the mouth and we monitored them from a close distance (see Chapter 4 for considerations about children's ability to evaluate risk). In response Leonor (two years old) decided to grasp the mushrooms with the help of kitchen tongs. The challenge of grabbing the small mushroom mobilised her fine motor skills and also required great concentration and persistence. Figures 3.9a–b show Leonor trying to grab the small mushroom and smelling it in order to develop a deeper knowledge about it.

Figures 3.9a–b Wild mushrooms can be dangerous. Proper support from the adult is crucial to guarantee children learn how to stay safe, without needing to be forbidden from exploring and playing.

The children collected parts of the different species they found and took them inside for future explorations (e.g. looking at the mushrooms through a magnifying glass). During the following day, every time we were outside, the children searched for the mushrooms, expressing their curiosity about the phenomenon. Diogo took the initiative to water the mushrooms as represented in Figure 3.10.

Figure 3.10 'I will water the mushrooms to make them grow!' – Through play Diogo shows an attitude of concern and care towards natural life.

Another example of how the weather can impact on play can be shared with the following experience. After several days of rain, the sun appeared on a beautiful autumn morning and prompted us to play outside. When we arrived in the garden, the children were surprised by all the yellow leaves that almost entirely covered the grass in the garden. Vicente (22 months old), who was still a bit insecure about walking, grasped the wooden fence to carefully explore the leaves. He was scared and uncomfortable with that situation, taking prudent steps and staying near a support. When I approached and suggested that he pick up some of the leaves, he was amazed by the crackling sound produced as the leaves broke into small pieces in his hands. Afterwards, I challenged him to try and break the leaves with his feet and he gradually began to take bigger and more confident steps, enjoying the sound produced. In this way his attention was on the noise his feet were making rather than his tentative walking skills. This lack of attention to the skill of walking meant, however, that he was more confident as he moved.

Spontaneously, different activities of interest started to emerge among the group. Some of the children ran and kicked the leaves, happy about the sound that the leaves made and the colours that flew into the air. Others were motivated to build big piles of leaves followed by scattering them as far and wide as possible. In Figure 3.11 Diogo is playing peekaboo with another child, using the leaf to hide his face.

We were amazed to realise how such simple things, such as dry leaves, promoted a wonderful play moment, where some children, like Vicente, were able to improve their confidence and self-esteem.

Figure 3.11 Play is the most natural activity for children. Children are creative and they find opportunities for play where we least expect it.

Water and soil – the top two ingredients of natural play

Talking about play in the natural world without mentioning activities related to water and soil would be a significant flaw. Water and soil can be understood as fundamental elements of the outdoors, creating the opportunities for learning across different areas of development.

Experiencing direct contact with soil is something that captivates and engages children in an intense way. Marcos (24 months old) deeply enjoyed playing with mud and showed high levels of involvement with this activity on several occasions. He truly engaged in the task of filling and emptying different receptacles with soil and water, never showing any signs of boredom or distraction. He was completely disconnected from what the others around him were doing, maintaining his full attention on the activity. As he switched some of the receptacles he used to collect the mud in, he was able to gather information about their characteristics (e.g. how long it took to fill a large pot, how to get the soil into a bottle with a narrow neck). While he was playing, his expression showed signs of happiness and serenity and he accepted other children joining him in his play (see Figure 3.12).

Figure 3.12 Playing with water and soil is one of the most captivating activities for young children outside.

As children played in groups they were able to organise themselves according to different tasks. Some of them were in charge of putting the soil into the plastic containers; others went to get water, so they could produce mud. There were still those who preferred to gather herbs or other elements to introduce into the mud mixture. From time to time, they exchanged utensils and dropped the containers, without coming into conflict with each other or experiencing frustration. The activity was absorbing for the action itself, the process being all important and not the product or outcome. Figure 3.13

Figure 3.13 Simple and easy-to-find resources can promote and improve mud play. With enough materials children are more willing to share and cooperate.

represents the group interaction. This brings us to the centrality of having enough resources and containers so that the children can organise themselves in a way that each one has their own space and responsibility (see Chapter 7 to know more about providing challenging outdoor play materials for children).

Playing with water and soil also allows children to be amazed by the environment. When I showed Xavier and Daniel that the small rocks disappeared in the puddle of muddy water, they were impressed by the 'magic' and wanted to try for themselves. They decided to put so many rocks in the puddle that gradually the rocks started to appear, since the amount of water could not cover them anymore. Trying to demonstrate the opposite phenomenon (floating), I took all the rocks out and put a small plastic cap in the puddle, which floated. I asked the children why the cap did not disappear and immediately Daniel answered: 'It's a boat!' Afterwards, we did several experiments with different objects, introducing progressively the concept of floating.

The significance of the water was also evident when the children had the opportunity to jump in the puddles. Tirelessly, they stamped their feet with such joy, enjoying the various splashes of water, regardless of how wet they got. Much of their enjoyment and desire to repeat the movement came from the power they felt impacting something else in such a spectacular way. In Figure 3.14 children are playing with the muddy water that remained inside a bucket. They exhibited delight as the splashes of water reach their faces.

Another example of the centrality of water and soil is illustrated in the following example. After days of rain the children discovered that the garden tunnels were filled with muddy water. With the rain, the structure inspired a renewed interest, encouraging different play activities. Some children ran inside the tunnels, laughing as they enjoyed the effect produced (see Figure 3.15). Others threw various objects such as pebbles and small sticks, becoming intrigued when they disappeared, submerged in water.

Figure 3.14 Two children who rarely played together inside found a common interest in the outdoor area.

Figure 3.15 Enjoying the consequences of the rain.

Among the children, Xavier's play stood out, as he painted the white walls of the tunnel with his hands filled with mud. Enthused by his discovery he said: 'I'm painting!' transforming the white walls into a huge screen, where he could express himself, using broad and energetic movements. Figure 3.16 illustrates this and we highlight the admiration of the other children observing Xavier. This situation showed us how activities such as writing, painting or drawing, often connected more to the inside classroom, can also be developed outside, allowing for different learning opportunities.

Related to this experience of Xavier's, painting on the blackboard with different objects and in different ways was an activity that also captivated the children. With adult support, they noticed that the water left marks on the blackboard, darkening its surface, as ink does on paper. Wetting their hands in the rain puddles the children used them to make drawings on the board. Daniel painted his hand several times, tracing it in a gentle and careful way, as he commented: 'This is Daniel's hand. Two hands of Daniel!' (see Figure 3.17).

Figure 3.16 In the outdoors children can express themselves in different ways. An activity such as painting with mud on a big surface is something that cannot be reproduced inside.

Figure 3.17 As Daniel makes a handprint on the board he is exploring notions of representation and abstraction, crucial concepts for future learning.

When the exploration of the body as a painting instrument stopped being something new, children then started to use leaves, sticks or tree branches, enjoying the effect of the different objects on the board's surface. With several tries, they started to understand that the leaves produced small spots on the board, breaking down very easily as they were handled. The tree branches filled the frame with splashes whenever the children shook them vigorously. And the sticks allowed a greater control over what they intended to represent, resembling a brush or pencil. In Figure 3.18 one of the boys is using a paint brush and the other one is using a stick.

With a strong desire to experiment and innovate, Diogo stood out from the rest of the group, as he decided to use an orange as a painting instrument, showing a divergent innovative way of thinking (see Figure 3.19).

Figure 3.18 Finding different uses for natural materials through experimentation.

Figure 3.19 Outdoor play promotes inquisitive children – children that are never satisfied and always want to find new solutions.

In this activity, with adult support, the interest in letters and numbers also emerged, since the children started to recognise and be able to draw letters from their names. Figures 3.20a–b represent other moments when children started to use different materials to draw or represent letters.

Figures 3.20a–b Leonor is representing the letter 'X' with sticks and Xavier is using the rope as a paint brush. Through play and without being pressured by the adult, children start to become aware of the written word.

Collecting minibeasts and plants

As tireless explorers, children are constantly making discoveries in the outdoors, finding many things that sometimes go unnoticed to the adult's eye. From colourful flowers, sticks with odd shapes to shining pebbles, every find is considered a treasure that is worth saving. For example, in Figure 3.21 Leandro is playing with bay leaves and other herbs pretending to be cooking. He relates the smell of the bay leaves to food and he enjoys using them in his play.

Aware of this interest to discover natural life and trying to support it, we decided to introduce a more challenging dimension to the collection impetus, giving scissors to the children, so they could gather different types of plants. The scissors were received by the group with great excitement, since they felt proud to be able to use something that is normally reserved for adults.

Figure 3.21 Through pretend play children can represent familiar situations and gain new knowledge about objects, situations and actions.

Using the scissors demanded a good deal of focus and coordination. The children needed to position and angle the blades of the scissors correctly between the thin stem of the plant and have the strength to cut the plant, without getting injured. For the small hands of Diogo, who was only two years old, the task was truly fascinating. In his expression we could see his eyes focused and a precise body posture (see Figure 3.22). This child was displaying many of the Laevers attributes of involvement such as concentration, persistence, motivation, energy, creativity and fascination (Laevers 2003). (See Chapter 6 for a more detailed discussion of Laevers's work.) This child was committed to the challenge and every time he was able to cut a plant, a feeling of joy and success emerged on his face.

Figure 3.22 Adults' intervention is important to expand and enrich children's play. Apart from promoting different skills, giving scissors to the children was important to build their self-esteem and confidence.

While some children were playing with the scissors, Marcos found a set of dried herbs in the ground. He ran towards me holding the herbs and saying that it was a bird's nest. He was fascinated with his discovery, pointing to the sky with excitement, where we could see some birds flying. He treated the supposed nest with great care and he decided to put it in the branches of a tree in the garden. Together, we considered the best position for the nest, in order to be sure that it would not fall. He also decided to make it more comfortable, adding small pieces of plants that he cut with the help of the scissors. Acknowledging Marcos's excitement, other children wanted to help him. Marcos was happy to cooperate with his friends and the task of improving the nest created a good opportunity for teamwork and group creativity. Matilde cut and carried small bundles of herbs, Marcos put them in the nest, Daniel made sure they were in the correct position and Valéria trimmed the unaligned ends with scissors. In Figures 3.23a–c it is possible to see how the group of two-year-old children cooperated to achieve a shared goal.

Figures 3.23a–c Children mobilised their knowledge about birds' nests when they were using the scissors. The ability to transfer learning from different situations shows great insight. The shared goal to create a good nest for the bird also represents a caring attitude towards animals.

The natural world is all around us and even in an urban area there is always some greenery, and often surprisingly more than we at first think. The natural world is there, it is free and it is ever changing. We need to be ready to take advantage of it to help children as they learn to understand the world and themselves.

Myths about under threes

Young children cannot focus on one activity for a long time

Quite often we hear people underestimating young children, by saying that they cannot focus on the same activity for a long period of time. Although we acknowledge differences in the attention spans between under threes and older children, we are driven to argue that those differences are not as deep as sometimes it is suggested. Through the experiences reported in this chapter we aim to deconstruct this myth, as we have come to realise that if the environment is right and the adult creates a supportive atmosphere for children to be engaged in, responding to their interests and needs, good concentration levels will be achieved. When we observe a child playing with mud, as we described with Marcos, we understand that time is an important factor in guaranteeing his attention. It is important that Marcos knows that he will have the time to invest in his play and that he can remain playing for the next few hours or days. Moreover, Marcos had the necessary tools to progressively expand his play and he knew that the adults understood the importance of the activity to him.

4 | Becoming safe through taking risks

Figure 4.0 Outdoor play allows children to explore their own limits and to overcome barriers.

Summary

In our current society risk is understood as something that must be regulated, evaluated, managed or even removed, in favour of children's protection and security. The centrality of risky play as an important trigger for children's development is often ignored, with a strong risk avoidance approach, which supports a culture of fear in what concerns the safety of the youngest child (Gill 2010; RoSPA 2016). In this chapter we define what we mean by risk, look at the research associated with risk and finally share some examples of children approaching risky situations and overcoming them. The role of the adult as well as the dilemmas they could face are considered.

Defining risk

Recognising that the word 'risk' can be applied in a variety of contexts, it is important to clarify the meaning that is attributed in this book. For Little and Eager (2010), risk is present in situations that involve the need to make choices between different ways of action, without knowing the outcome. It can be understood as a continuum that is not necessarily associated with negative consequences. From the perspective of these authors, risk can be distinguished from danger, a notion that is applied in situations when the probability of hazard is high, leading to serious injuries or death. The discourse that surrounds us tends to focus on the darker side of risk – seeing the uncertainty, the possibility of failure, of injury. As teachers, however, it is important that we ensure that the positive aspects of risk are acknowledged – the possibility of discovering that one is adventurous, daring, brave, strong, confident and successful (Stephenson 2003, p. 42; Sandseter 2009).

In this book, risky play is understood as an opportunity for children to test limits, to face challenges and to try new experiences, dealing with the possibility of accidents (Ball 2002; Stephenson 2003). Risky play can be described as a type of physical activity that can be emotional, enthusiastic, scary and uncertain, engaging children in the search for adventures in their daily lives (Sandseter 2010; Smith 1998).

In the research developed by Sandseter (2007), risky play can be defined by six main features – play with high speed; play with great heights; use of dangerous tools; play near dangerous elements; possibility of disappearance or getting lost; and rough and tumble play. Blurton-Jones (1967, p. 355) categorised the eight movement patterns that are present when children are playing rough and tumble. These are: running, chasing and felling, wrestling, jumping up and down with both feet together, beating at each other with an open hand without actually hitting, beating at each other with an object but not hitting, laughing and sometimes falling and throwing the body onto the ground. The research by Holland (2003) demonstrates how trying to demonise rough and tumble play actually causes great problems for young children and they will try to play despite the rules. Blatchford, Pellegrini and Baines (2016) indicate that rough and tumble play is an important part of childhood as children are learning social skills and in particular learning to read others' non-verbal actions. Furthermore, it can be a competitive construct, where children learn how to get on while discovering the dynamics of groups and group cohesion – who are the leaders and followers.

Each risky situation provides high levels of positive stimulation and promotes feelings of happiness, enthusiasm, pride, fear and anxiety (in Figure 4.1 the excitement and joy are triggered by running at high speed). Although apparently contradictory, the mixture of feelings can be understood as a possible explanation for why risk is so captivating for children (Apter 2007). As Pellegrini (2009) argues, children like the sense of unpredictability in play.

Adults' perception of risk

According to Adams (2002), the notion of risk is related to a subjective dimension, linked to the person who analyses the situation. In this way risk cannot be measured or quantified. Each person will understand risk in a unique and distinct way, depending on the interpretation of individual experiences. As adults caring for young children it is us who will make the environment challenging and exciting or simple and undemanding. Waller and colleagues indicated that whether we allow risk or not will be based on our values and how we view the child. If we see the child as 'competent' then we will provide a challenging environment, whereas if we view them as 'vulnerable' then we will consider our role as one of protection and provide an undemanding environment (Waller, Sandseter, Wyver, Ärlemalm Hagsér & Maynard 2010, p. 441). However, we cannot allow our unconscious bias to close down an important aspect of children's development and we have to regularly make a 'values audit' or check our 'value position' (Pollard 2008, p. 125), as this

Figure 4.1 Running as a way to express energy, excitement and joy.

acts as a measuring tool, to check if we are being consistent within our school setting, to check external pressures and to check our actual practice. Figure 4.2 shows how risky play can be integrated in the child–adult relationship. With adult support and encouragement children feel progressively more confident to face challenges independently.

Figure 4.2 Attentive adults can promote risky play, acknowledging children's interests and skills.

Apart from having a strong subjective dimension, risk can also be understood as an interactive phenomenon, in which the experiences, feelings and opinions of others influence the perception of the situation. The characteristics of the society and culture in which we exist also have a significant influence on the way children and adults manage and understand risk (Sandseter 2010).

Why risk is important

Risky play has an important role in child development, responding to his/her natural curiosity and need for stimulation. Facing challenging situations allows for the improvement of skills related to risk evaluation and management, which implies the analysis of personal and environmental characteristics. In this way, the child acquires a greater familiarity with contexts, redefines expectations and knowledge about their capabilities and limits, applies problem-solving strategies and rehearses useful skills, in order to become progressively independent towards adulthood (Ball 2002; Gill 2010; Sandseter 2010). Through risky play experiences, the child learns how to deal with fear, gains a greater knowledge about action outcomes and develops confidence to make decisions. Climbing up a tree, as shown in Figure 4.3, represents a great adventure for a two-year-old, demanding an assessment of risk and individual skills.

Figure 4.3 'Am I capable of climbing up the tree?' Facing risks improves body knowledge and awareness.

The disposition to deal with risk is also related to the capability and motivation to learn, which involves security, competence and the will to succeed. Stephenson (2003) suggests that there is a relationship between children's success in overcoming obstacles outside and their motivation to accept challenges in other areas. The experience of risky adventures allows for the expansion of personal barriers (physical, cognitive, emotional) in a controlled and supportive environment, in which the possibility of error is expected and accepted (Waite 2011). Also, the interaction with risk promotes the acquisition of attitudes of persistence and entrepreneurship, leading to the interpretation of problems as challenges, in which it is possible to practise the unexpected and to enjoy the process of problem solving (Gill 2010; Stephenson 2003). Figure 4.4 illustrates a situation in which the children, without adult help, were able to find a suitable strategy to use the climbing wall. They used a plastic crate to achieve the first footholds and they ventured to climb to the top.

Figure 4.4 Children seek challenges and are creative in finding the best strategies to solve them.

As RoSPA (2016) argue, it is naïve and unrealistic to believe that it is possible to abolish all forms of risk. In children's daily lives risk is always present and it is not possible or desirable to keep them in a bubble-wrapped environment. It is important to create spaces that allow for risky experiences, aware of danger but also aware that an excess of security can be harmful to children. Indeed, both the Royal Society for the Prevention of Accidents (RoSPA 2016) and the Health and Safety Executive (HSE 2016) argue that children need to face and overcome challenges and that risk is an important life learning tool. RoSPA (2016) maintain that children playing outside will support strong mental and physical health and well-being. Scratched knees or elbows are signs of childhood, representing important experiences of learning through trial and error (see Figure 4.5).

Figure 4.5 During risky play small accidents can happen. Absolute safety is not possible or desirable.

The close relationship between context and subject emphasises the need to listen to children (Rose and Rogers 2012), seeking to understand what structures and activities they prefer. What is considered as a challenge for some children may not apply to others, being necessary to adapt the risky experiences according to different levels of development. The need for balance in the type of risks that the environment offers demands a flexible attitude, through which it is possible to distinguish which activities represent a reasonable level of risk for one child but are too dangerous for others (Ball 2002; Stephenson 2003).

The risky play experiences reported in this chapter involve children between twenty-four and thirty-six months old, for whom risky play is perceived according to their age and stage of development.

Children's and adults' stories – theory into action

To see the world from a higher level

The tree house

In our garden there is a beautiful plum tree, with strong branches, which supports a small wooden house. The house is located more than two metres above the ground and the only way to get inside is through a steep and narrow stepladder. In a phase of development when motor coordination is not completely acquired, going up the tree house steps is a major challenge that generates adrenaline and insecurity.

For Vicente, twenty-four months old, going up into the tree house was a demanding and long-lasting task, marked by several episodes of failure. One day, after observing other children from the group going up to and down from the tree house, showing signs of happiness and enjoyment, Vicente felt ready to try for himself. In the beginning, every time he climbed onto the first step he was overtaken by another child, thereby holding back his attempt to succeed.

In this situation, I realised that it was necessary to intervene and to encourage Vicente to continue, without being dominated by his inner insecurity and demotivation. At a certain point, when the children had stopped racing round to climb the steps, I suggested to Vicente that he might try one more time to go into the tree house, keeping myself close by to support him. Starting to climb, he showed signs of tension and anxiety, and his eyes were focused, alternately, on my face and on the steps, searching for the support needed to accomplish this mission. When he started to get close to the top of the steps, his facial expression changed and the tension was substituted by a big smile. At the top, he clapped his hands and laughed, showing happiness. Acknowledging his victory, I invited all the children to congratulate Vicente for his effort and persistence. The group clapped and shouted his name!

The great height of the tree house demanded caution and attention from the children, as they climbed up and down the structure. With time and practice, each child developed strategies and acquired more agility and precise movements. Vincent, for example, started to gradually use his body to adapt to the different challenges. Initially, he climbed up the stairs with his hands and knees based on the structure and went down using a sitting position. After a few days of practice he was able to go up and down standing up in both directions, showing a more calm and secure attitude towards the task. With time, he found ways to increase the challenge, so he started to carry objects to the tree house and up the stairs (see Figures 4.6a–b).

Figures 4.6a–b Children never stop looking for new adventures. Through practice and persistence challenges become easier and a need for more complex and difficult situations emerge.

Apart from the challenges related to the height, the tree house also offered other types of risky play experiences, such as the possibility of being away from the adult's sight. In the spring, the trees become greener, with dense foliage, creating a good hiding space, where children can be away from what could be construed as controlling eyes. Inside the tree house different dialogues, play activities and games happen, creating the necessary conditions for trusting and learning among peers.

Going up and down the hill

The hill created in the garden of the setting can be considered to be one of the main areas of interest outside. Because of its large size (a dome two metres high by five metres wide) several children can use it at the same time, developing different strategies and motor skills to arrive at the top. The sides of the hill are significantly steep, and the ground can become slippery. The hill is made up of plants, soil and rocks and this creates a challenging environment for the children as they go up and down. In Figures 4.7a–b the enjoyment and the challenge offered by the hill are illustrated.

Figures 4.7a–b Children mobilised different strategies to go up and down the hill. The social interaction in this situation, as children helped and challenged each other, made it more interesting and captivating.

Thinking back to the learning experience in the tree house, we found it possible to identify different attitudes towards risk. Tomás and Leonor, for example, quickly felt very comfortable in dealing with the climbing challenge. Although they went through a learning period, in which they used their hands to climb up and sat down to go back down, this was only necessary for a few days of practice before they were able to feel confident enough to go up and down standing up. Figure 4.8 represents the first time Tomás was able to climb up the hill without any help. When he arrived to the top we celebrated his achievement, both feeling happy and excited. This situation is a good example of how risky play can be encouraged and shared between children and adults.

Once they arrived at the top of the hill, the children noticeably appreciated the surrounding landscape. Tomás liked to see the primary school, which his older cousin attended. Leonor searched on the horizon for the farm where we used to go and talked about the sunset. Both children (two years old) were highly empathetic towards the other children as they tried to help them climb up to the top of the hill. They shared tips about the best strategy to adopt, offering helpful advice: 'Give me your hand, I'll pull you up' and tried to motivate them with words of encouragement: 'You can do it!' (see Figure 4.9).

From a different perspective, however, Matilde (two years old) was restless and uncomfortable with the obstacles presented by the hill, showing signs of disappointment and sadness. She was still insecure about controlling her body and she gave up very easily every time she faced a barrier. Acknowledging the need to support Matilde in overcoming that challenge, we started to develop some initiatives in order to promote her confidence. We encouraged her to imitate more skilful peers and every time she tried to climb the hill by herself the entire group celebrated her attempt. Gradually, with adult and peer support, she improved her sense of control over the situation and started to be

Figure 4.8 Feeling proud and happy for having succeeded in something difficult is one of the most positive consequences of risky play.

Figure 4.9 Risky play situations offer good conditions for learning among peers. Children enjoy helping each help other as they easily understand the difficulties experienced by others.

able to deal with that challenge in a positive way. In Figure 4.10 it is possible to see young Matilde looking back, searching for help and encouragement. As time went by, going up and down the hill became an activity very much appreciated by the little girl. The fear and the discomfort were substituted by a sense of success and conquering of personal barriers, which contributed to the development of a positive self view.

Figure 4.10 Challenges are interpreted differently by each child. Respecting the child's rhythm is an important dimension when promoting risky play.

This situation also made it possible to understand that the skills for overcoming these obstacles and the ability to deal with risk are related to a learning process, rather than an assessable outcome that does not occur in an immediate way. In order to master a certain skill or challenge, several experiences across different periods of time are needed. At a particular point during the year, the children stopped going to the hill, due to bad weather conditions. This situation generated insecurity and discomfort among the group as they reencountered the hill a few weeks later. But being aware of the need for repetition and the embedding of the schema we then allowed the children to experiment and experience so that again they reached a high level of security with that particular skill.

There is always a first time

The ability for children to face new challenges, testing skills and overcoming fears, evolves so rapidly and unpredictably that it often surprises adults. A good example of this was when two young boys started to climb up the ramp, without showing any fear or hesitation. Older children (from four to ten years old) normally used this structure, but the two-year-olds had never tried it before. The ramp is fixed to the boundary wall of the outdoor space and is quite high (around two metres) and steep, offering some risk due to the possibility of falling (see Figure 4.11a).

Taken by surprise, we were apprehensive about this situation, without knowing what the best thing to do was. We knew that we should not let our own fears undermine the experimenting by the children, so we decided to get closer to the climbing frame, observing the children but keeping the necessary distance to give a sense of autonomy and freedom. It was with great interest that we tracked the children, realising the level of motor coordination, agility and strength both boys showed. When they reached the top of the ramp they were very excited, particularly by what they could see from their vantage point. The boys started to call other children and adults to share their achievement and for many minutes we talked with them about what they could see – people working in the fields, the dogs barking and the birds flying in the sky. Figure 4.11b shows the children at the top of the ramp, admiring what was behind the setting boundaries.

Out of the adult's sight

The visits to the setting's farm can be described as authentic adventures that promoted different skills and learning opportunities. Going out of the controlled and familiar space of the setting with a group of two-year-olds can be described as a tough challenge that demands a careful risk assessment and the development of preventive strategies (e.g. avoiding areas with more traffic). On the walk to the farm (around 500 metres) we drew children's attention to different stimuli, such as cars, tractors, herds, motorbikes, dogs, among other things. These points of interest, apart from having some risk associated, also promoted several dialogues and instigated an attitude of curiosity and questioning among the children. Figures 4.12a–b exemplify some of those experiences.

As we arrived at the farm, different challenges were presented to the children, since they had a big area to explore, with several animals and plants. The majority of the children (from 24 to 36 months old) happily walked around the farm, feeling able to discover new spaces and getting out of the adult's view, as Figure 4.13 shows.

Vicente often stayed near the lake, hanging over the fence to see the frogs jumping into the water. Other times he walked along the potato patch, where he knew that we could find small beetles that tickled his hands. Alice enjoyed going to the greenhouse to collect fresh tomatoes. Leandro often spent a lot of time finding snails, walking long distances by himself, without being affected if he fell over. He was one of the younger children in the

Figure 4.11a 'They can fall! What happens if they fall?' The adult has to control his/her personal fears and evaluate the risky situations from the child's perspective.

Figure 4.11b Risk allows for new discoveries about the world.

Figure 4.12a The lady was watering the garden and the children took the opportunity to cool off.

Figure 4.12b The encounter with the goats was an unexpected surprise. Despite the risk involved, the children showed no fear and approached the animals with enthusiasm.

Figure 4.13 It is important for children to be able to move away from the adult, showing confidence and autonomy. Keeping a distance does not mean that they cannot return or ask for help whenever they need.

group (26 months old) and walking on the uneven ground of the farm was a big challenge for him (see Figure 4.14a). He treated small animals and plants with care and he observed them closely, without being distracted by the surroundings (in Figure 4.14b it is possible to identify signs of concentration and amazement in Leandro's expression). Tomás and Marcos usually chose the strawberry patch as their preferred play space. They filled small plastic bags with the fruits they picked and they tried to make sure that each of them had equal quantities.

Figures 4.14a–b Leandro showed persistence and determination as he walked in the farm. Because he felt motivated and stimulated by the environment, falling did not discourage him from achieving his goals.

With these examples we want to demonstrate that gradually each child gained the confidence to discover their own areas of interest, exploring the surroundings in small groups or individually. The children knew that adults would always be there to support them, even though they could be what felt like far away, or out of their sight. Equally, we want to demonstrate that children need to be given time to acclimatise to a new space, particularly if they have no experience of the space (e.g. farms, woodland, rivers). Sometimes adults can misinterpret children's reticence in a new space as fear, whereas it is simply a case of making themselves familiar with it.

Using swords and guns

The experiences related to rough and tumble play should be understood in a flexible way, recognising its importance for the development of social, motor and emotional skills. Through play fighting and chasing games children gain a greater knowledge about their body, using it to express emotions and desires. They learn how to interpret social signs and to find strategies to interact with others. Rough and tumble play allows for the development of skills related to creativity and imagination, as children assume different roles in play and redefine the use of objects to give coherence to their stories (e.g. a stick can be used as a sword). In Figures 4.15a–b the two boys gave a different meaning to the stick. In one case the stick was a weapon to fight the monsters and in the other case the stick was a tool to measure the height of the tree.

Among the group of children whose experiences are reported in this book, rough and tumble play was more apparent among boys. Frequently, sticks were used as swords or pistols, as they pretended to be cowboys or superheroes. In their play they tried to recreate stories or films they knew, getting more excited as the play became more adventurous (see Figures 4.16a–c). Girls' involvement in this type of play was limited to chasing games, in which they spontaneously switched roles of chaser and chased.

In most cases of rough and tumble play it was evident to the adults that the children were competent enough to deal with the situations. On several occasions we had the opportunity to realise that rough and tumble play was not necessarily linked to aggressive or socially inadequate behaviours, but an important strategy for children to learn and develop.

Figures 4.15a–b How exciting and stimulating can a stick be?

Figures 4.16a–c Play fighting should be understood as an important activity for children to express themselves and interact with others.

When the risk is not worth taking

Finding new places to play, taking advantage of the opportunities offered in the community, became a growing concern as the children started to show signs of having lost interest in relation to the outdoor space of the setting. The surprise and the pleasure associated with exploring unfamiliar environments turned the walks within the community area into rich learning experiences that strengthened the relationship of complicity between adults and children and also created new risky challenges, as the following example demonstrates. The children had the opportunity to play in a forest area that had a river running through it with some deep slopes to it. The riverside was not protected and had a steep bank down to the waterline, as represented in Figures 4.17a–b.

Figures 4.17a–b Both adults and children must be comfortable with risky situations. There are risks that are not worth taking.

We talked with the group about the danger of the area and we asked them to stay away from it. However, the children had a strong interest in the water and they quickly started to develop play activities that got them closer and closer to the riverside (e.g. throwing sticks or stones into the water). Facing this situation, the adults became anxious, fearing the occurrence of accidents. The interaction with the children changed to one of reprimands. Acknowledging the attractiveness of that space, we stayed there for some time. However, the anxiety shared among the adults undermined the adult involvement and the openness to explore the environment with the children.

If we assume that a space can only be good for the children if it is also good for the adults, we can regard the area's pedagogical potential as insufficient reason to stay there, as it was causing anxiety in the adults. Recognising the importance of risky play does not mean an unconditional acceptance of it, as it is necessary to consider different factors influencing the situation. Every activity should be considered carefully to judge whether it continues or has to be limited in some way.

Myths about under threes

Children are not capable of evaluating risk

Understanding the importance of risky play for learning and development is associated with the recognition of children's competence to evaluate situations and make judgements about the best strategies to adopt (Smith 1998). The research developed by Sandseter (2010) with preschool children and the work of Green and Hart (1998) with seven- and eleven-year-olds, both support the idea that children are aware of risk, adapting their behaviour according to the situation. In the research developed by Green and Hart (1998) the participants defended the importance of personal experience as an important source of information over formal advice provided by adults. Apart from that, security was interpreted as something related to individual responsibility, without implying the need for spaces with zero risk. From the data collected, Green and Hart (1998) were able to conclude that living adventures and challenges can be understood as something that belongs to a peer culture, characterising an important dimension of childhood. The study developed by Christensen and Mikkelsen (2008) supports this line of thought, since the data retrieved show that children between ten and twelve years old are not only able to evaluate their personal skills and limits, but also accept different levels of risk tolerance among their peers. In the observations conducted by the researchers, it was possible to notice that children discussed play rules, aiming to find a level of risk that was accepted by all group members. In this situation, the children showed an attitude of empathy, cooperation and respect for different perspectives about risk, gaining a better knowledge about the most appropriate skills to deal with the situation. From this perspective, Christensen and Mikkelsen (2008) considered that 'although children may make misjudgements, they do not, as it is sometimes assumed, "blindly" throw themselves into risk-taking behaviours' (p. 16). In the experiences reported we also can see that from an early age children are aware of risk and they are capable of evaluating their skills according to the situation. In the episodes shared about the tree house or the hill, for example, we can assume that both Vicente and Matilde were aware of the risk and that was why they felt scared to try the experiences. Also, the other children were very understanding and they tried to support their friends as best they could.

Every time a child faces a problem the adult should immediately help

Adult evaluation about risky play situations and their own predispositions to deal with risk has a great influence on the type of challenges that are provided for children (Sandseter 2009). When the adult is capable of managing risk in a flexible way, recognising its positive impact for children's development, it is possible to assume that challenging experiences will be promoted. Risky play experiences demand reflections about the adult role, considering that their participation can either disturb the child or give an important support to overcome an obstacle. When an adult intervenes unnecessarily he/she may send a message of distrust that makes the child feel insecure and frustrated. However, when the adult help occurs in a situation in which the child is suffering or struggling too much to succeed, a sensitive and supportive intervention is crucial to help the child deal with the experience. If we think about the situation when the two boys climbed the ramp for the first time, we can easily understand that sometimes it is important to let children deal with the challenges on their own, otherwise they will not feel the sense of success and accomplishment in overcoming the task. It is important to make sure that adults' feelings of anxiety do not undermine the children's involvement.

Stephenson's research (2003) indicated that the interest of the children towards physical challenges is in great part supported by the educators' attitude towards risk and not so much by the equipment characteristics. In the observed settings, professionals enjoyed being outside, appreciated activities that involved physical activity and showed a sensitive and liberal approach towards children's supervision. They allowed children to face risks and challenging experiences, without putting them in dangerous situations (Stephenson 2003).

It is important to notice that the need to give space to children to allow them to test their limits and to make decisions about their skills and interests does not negate or undervalue the importance of the adult role as an observer or a participant in the risky experience. As Tovey (2007) suggests, although children should have opportunities to learn how to evaluate and manage risk, the lack of life experiences they have had thus far emphasises the need for adult support.

5 Companionship and shared experiences

Figure 5.0 Childhood memories should be filled with moments of happiness and pleasure.

Summary

The development of close relationships between quite young children and adults in the natural outdoor environment is the main focus of this chapter. Moments of sharing, cooperation and empathy are described, contradicting the assumption that young children are solitary players. From simple experiences such as observing the horizon in the company of friends (see Figure 5.1) to more elaborated play activities, where negotiation and problem solving were required, the experiences shared in the outdoor area allowed children to gain a greater knowledge about themselves and others, contributing to the development of strong emotional bonds among the group (children and adults).

Figure 5.1 Admiring the sky and the view in the company of others.

Social development

The outdoors can be understood as a rich social environment, where children have the possibility to interact with others in different ways. Opportunities for social development often emerge due to the dynamic of the space, which offers surprises and challenges for children to overcome. In an unpredictable scenario, adults are not able to control or intervene simultaneously in multiple situations, so cooperation among children arises as a spontaneous solution to achieve play goals. In Figures 5.2a–b the two young girls work together to be successful in the task of moving the log. From the figure it is possible to acknowledge that challenges gain a new meaning when faced with peers, enabling children to learn how to manage with unanticipated and unknown situations of adulthood (RoSPA 2016).

Figures 5.2a–b Together we are stronger!

Figure 5.3 Learning goes beyond scholarly knowledge and it is also about understanding the needs and perspectives of others.

Children become teachers and learners, as they benefit from or give help to others, taking advantage of their abilities and previous experiences. In the situations reported below it is possible to notice that children enjoy feeling useful and are eager to share knowledge and skills. In Figure 5.3, for example, the young girl shows a kind attitude towards the boy, giving him water and helping with the cup.

However, cooperation is not a simple process for young children as it demands most importantly an understanding of empathy – we have to understand the other person's point of view, which then involves the skills of negotiation, compromise and context evaluation. Developing an attitude of empathy and care about others is something that takes time and multiple experiences, so children can progressively comprehend the complex features of human socialisation. Outside, children are gradually confronted with opportunities to practise social skills, as they have the opportunity to interact with peers in a more relaxed environment than inside, being able to choose moments to connect with others or to play individually, without having to continually run into each other as so often happens in the classroom.

A dynamic and enabling environment

Being able to accept other peoples' ideas and respect different interests and needs is something that requires practice, and it can be achieved if children feel good with themselves and others. To foster cooperation amongst a group of young children it is necessary to create an enabling environment. This means children need time to get to know the outdoor environment well by visiting it every day. Enough space (the younger the child, the more space they need) and sufficient resources and materials for all the children should be provided by adults that recognise the rich potential of the natural world.

Figures 5.4a–b represents an episode of cooperation and mutual understanding that only occurred because children were given time and adequate resources to play with.

Figure 5.4a 'Put a bit more water here,' said Valéria. 'OK. Can you put some in mine?' asked Daniel.

Figure 5.4b The two children spent more than 30 minutes talking and exchanging water from one container to another. Adults did not interfere and no conflicts occurred.

Shared understanding

The experiences reported below aim to show how outdoor play experiences can have an impact on the relationships between children and adults. Outside, adults (from our experience) feel more relaxed and available to connect with the children, being open to new ways of doing and learning. Through outdoor play interactions adults and children show a different 'self' from the one that acts inside, promoting the possibility of getting to know each other on a deeper level. Children can quite literally change as they move into the outdoor area, feeling more confident, comfortable and unjudged (Bilton 2010).

In open spaces, adults can walk slowly with a small group of children or just one child, stopping to observe, comment and appreciate the natural world. This level of connectedness can mean the development of a deep relationship with the child and thereby will help the adult to better understand and support learning (see Figures 5.5a–b, in which the adult is showing to one child the effect of the morning frost in the pine tree).

The adult has the important role of putting into words children's perceptions and feelings, supporting the development of a sense of pleasure and gratification towards learning (Mendonça 2014; Portugal, Carvalho & Bento n.d.). The process of education becomes central rather than the outcome, which is so often valued inside the classroom. Finally, the outdoors can provide moments of intense pleasure and stimulation, when children, teachers, parents and others participate as learners in a co-constructed environment (Mendonça 2014).

Figures 5.5a–b With adult support children became aware of the multiple phenomena that occur in the natural world.

A sense of belonging and connectedness

The development of attitudes of companionship and empathy are also related to a sense of belonging and connectedness to a group of people and a space. Belonging – and therefore connectedness – is about being accepted, included and respected as a member of a group (Goodenow & Grady 1993) and it is naturally associated with feelings of concern for others, wishing for their well-being. Maslow (1962) stated that the need for belonging, which he joins with love, is crucial for human motivation and therefore development. Also, a large-scale research project has made a strong link between school engagement and long-term outcomes, with belongingness being a component of engagement (Abbott-Chapman, Martin, Ollington, Venn, Dwyer & Gall 2014).

The outdoor environment project reported in this book allowed children, staff and parents to develop a strong connection with each other, based on the positive and successful experiences that occurred outside. The children got to know each other very well, because they were playing closely and regularly together and also because they talked about each other as a group. The shared experiences of cooperation and problem solving help to establish preferable playmates, with whom the children feel secure and at ease. From an early age, friendships have an important role in the development of personality and self-esteem and interactions with peers bring important information for learning about each individual (see Figures 5.6a–b).

Figures 5.6a–b Peers as mirrors for the development of self-knowledge.

Part of belonging is sharing experiences that become stories to recount, be it a myth told and retold generationally or the story of an incident at the centre, such as having an overnight stay together. This deep connectedness to others is undoubtedly the essence of why these children were able at a young age to cooperate, to consider others and to care for all. These positive experiences with peers and adults will contribute to children being able to trust others and to empathise with their needs or difficulties as they grow older and face more intricate social situations.

Children's and adults' stories – theory into action

Building bridges

In the outdoors children share experiences, desires, interests and they gradually develop a sense of companionship expressed through play, as the following examples demonstrate. At a certain point in the year, some children were engaged in playing and learning about animals. In the outdoor area they enjoyed looking for minibeasts, showing surprise and wonder at ants, ladybugs, spiders and snails, as represented in Figure 5.7. They liked watching small videos and observing pictures of real animals, asking many questions about how they were, where they live, what they eat, etc. Following this interest we introduced small toy animals, with which children were very keen to play, both inside and outside (Figure 5.8 shows one of many play moments with the animals).

One day, two-year-old Diogo wanted to take the horse figure to the garden, choosing the toy as the playmate for the day. While Diogo played in the soil on his own, showing involvement and abstraction from what the other children were doing, the small animal stayed next to him and the young boy talked to it in an excitable way, describing what he was doing. The joy of Diogo drew the attention of Xavier, who tried to get close and

Figures 5.7 Sharing a discovery.

Figure 5.8 Young Matilde expressing her curiosity and thirst for learning.

participate in the play activity. Following the pretend stories that Diogo shared with the animal, Xavier added: 'That horse has a broken leg! Maybe he broke a bone while he was running. Now he can't walk.' Diogo laughed at the idea and gladly accepted Xavier into his play.

For a while the two boys stayed crouched down, digging a small hole in the ground and talking about animals. When the depth of the hole was satisfactory to them both, they ran in the direction of the water tank and from there, they carried a full watering can (adult size) together back to the play space. Due to the weight and size of the watering can Diogo and Xavier had to help each other in order to carry the water to the hole. In spite of the boys' effort, the water often spilled out onto the children's feet. They laughed, amused with the situation. The delay of getting the water to the hole did not upset them, as they rather seemed to take pleasure in the situation.

With the hole filled with water, the two-year-old boys plunged the plastic animals into the puddle. Suddenly, Diogo stopped what he was doing. It became apparent through his actions that he felt the horse could not go into the water given he had a broken leg. Diogo started to look around for a stick and asked Xavier to help him to look for one. The two boys moved away from the hole and started to investigate the ground. After a few minutes, they returned to the water with several small sticks in their hands. They knelt near to the hole and put two parallel sticks connecting the two banks of the puddle. With pride, Diogo told Xavier: 'See Xavier, in this way the horse can cross the river. It's a bridge!'

The two friends remained engaged in the play for a long time, talking with each other, cooperating and respecting each other's space and ideas. Between the boys there were no signs of conflict and there was an atmosphere of pure companionship.

Who is responsible for the watering can?

The outdoor area located in the backyard of the day care was a dynamic space, where the children could find several objects and structures for rich and challenging play (e.g. pots and pans, spoons, watering cans). Among the different stimuli, such as the hiding places or structures for climbing/jumping, this area was very attractive because it provided easy access to water and soil. Many exploratory games with these natural elements emerged in this place, as children played them with the help of open-ended resources. Through playing with mud, soil and water different opportunities for cooperation and socialisation emerged. One day, Tomás (33 months old), Alice (31 months old) and Leandro (24 months old) were playing with the water and grass, mixing it inside an old pan. With excitement and vigour they mixed the grass in the water, saying that they were washing it so they could eat the 'lettuce' afterwards (see Figure 5.9a). Leandro was the youngest in the group and he was very excited by the play. He looked up to the older children and as soon as he could he tried to imitate them. While the children were playing, Leonor (29 months old) was transporting water nearby and when she saw this small group, decided to join them on her own initiative, pouring the water she had into the container that the group was using (Figure 5.9b captured this moment).

The children were pleased to have more water to play with and gladly accepted Leonor into the activity. As they spilt the water onto the ground, Leonor quickly ran to the water tank to refill the can, feeling very proud with her responsibility and enjoying being useful to the others. Leandro observed Leonor with close attention and decided to copy what she was doing. He picked a big, heavy oven tray and started walking to the water tap with a determined attitude. However, he quickly realised that the tray was not an easy object to carry the water in and he started to look for another container. Acknowledging the difficulty faced by Leandro, Leonor helped the boy in his search and offered him a pan that she found. Demonstrating an empathetic and caring attitude, Leonor made it easy for the young boy to get engaged in the group activity and shared with him the responsibility of carrying the water for the rest of the children. They both felt that they had an important role in the play. Leonor was a mentor for Leandro and the young boy had the

Figures 5.9a–b Each child influences group play with their personality and view of the world.

opportunity to contribute to the play. In Figure 5.10 it is possible to observe Leandro achieving his goal, as he carries the pan of water. During this episode, it was never necessary for the adult to intervene. Although we were around and watching, the children did not call for our attention, as they showed competence to negotiate different roles and manage the resources during play.

Figure 5.10 With peer support learning gains a deeper meaning.

Family and friends

Playing mums and dads is an activity in which most children feel comfortable and at ease, as they bring to the play their own family experiences. This type of play often occurs in the more sheltered space of indoors, but the outdoors can also bring opportunities for companionship and sharing among the children.

One day in the backyard of the day care, Valéria and Leonor were playing inside a tent, hidden from the adult's sight (to better understand the area see Figure 5.11). They entered and left the tent several times, in order to fetch flowers, herbs and different objects.

A wooden plank represented a bed that they laid upon, as they hugged and giggled. The children were playing 'mum and daughter'. Valéria took care of her 'daughter' displaying gentleness and consideration, holding her hand as they moved around the space. Meanwhile, Leonor accepted the role of a loved baby, feeling pleased with the protection given by her 'mum'. In Figures 5.12a–b it is possible to see how delighted they both were, exchanging gestures of kindness and affection.

As the pretend play evolved, the girls switched roles and another child (Diogo) entered the story. The girls decided that Diogo should be the baby, Leonor the mum and Valéria was going to make soup for them all.

Figure 5.11 More secluded spaces promote social interaction between children.

Figures 5.12a–b Friendship is not determined by age. Empathy and care about others can be developed from birth.

Without wanting to disturb the children's play, I kept myself quiet and discreet as I observed that lovely moment. The interaction between the three children aged 29 and 30 months old showed the strong friendship and affection that they felt for each other. In our daily experiences in the setting it was frequent to see this group of children looking out for each other, trying to help and protect on different occasions. For example, in Figure 5.13 Leonor is cuddling Diogo as they both wake up after their nap. Their relationship was born in the setting and they had known each other since they were only a few months old. Despite their short lives, they had already shared many experiences of cooperation and kindness.

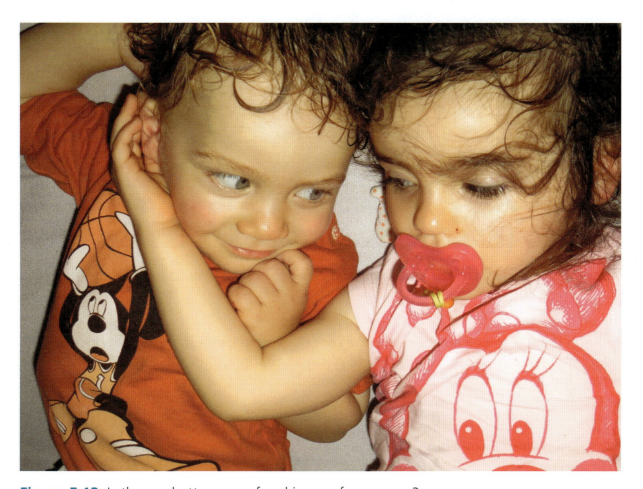

Figure 5.13 Is there a better way of waking up from a nap?

Guess who is...

Acknowledging the importance of organised routines to provide a sense of security and predictability to the children, every morning adults and children spent some minutes talking about the plans for the day or topics that children had in mind. Sitting on the floor or nestled on the sofa, in these moments children were stimulated to talk openly about their experiences, joys, fears or doubts. Subjects such as the birth of a brother, the headaches of a mum or the dog's visit to the vet were important conversational topics that were valued by the group and were meaningful for real language development. Figure 5.14 illustrates one of those moments, in which the meeting of the group happened outside and the children were talking and observing images of birds in a book.

Figure 5.14 Valuing children's opinions and experiences is crucial to supporting inquisitiveness and critical thinking.

From the several conversations we had over the year, the children gained a deep knowledge about each other and they were always very interested to know more. So, we developed a game that consisted of guessing the name of a person from the group by describing some of his/her physical and psychological characteristics. For example:

'Who is the boy that has short hair, likes to help others and loves to pick and eat strawberries from the greenhouse?'

'What is the name of the boy that is very gentle and enjoys playing with tools outside?'

Initially, it was always the adult who gave the clues for the child's identification but, with time, some children started to be able to create the riddles by themselves.

Diogo asked: 'Who is the girl that always gets very wet when playing with water and whose father is in Angola?'

All the children shouted: 'Valéria!'

With this simple activity and many group conversations, the children got to know characteristics, interests, likes and dislikes of each other.

Moreover, the strength of these relationships led to shared verbal expressions and signs that could be interpreted almost like a code within the group. Expressions of joy and charismatic phrases linked to past play experiences outside had a special meaning for us, contributing to the development of a strong group identity and sense of belonging. Figures 5.15a–d show signs of friendship, caring and closeness between the children.

Figure 5.15a Partners in many adventures and challenges.

Figure 5.15b Sharing misfortunes: Diogo is showing Tomás that he has a sore finger.

Figure 5.15c Young Alice is peeling the orange to give it to Leandro. A win-win situation, from which both children benefitted.

Figure 5.15d It is not always hugs and smiles. Sometimes conflicts emerge and children get hurt.

Adults as companions

The walks around the local area promoted important moments of companionship not only between the children, but between children and adults. The village pathways took us to beautiful places that allowed us to tell stories and traditions, such as the legend of the 'Enchanted Moorish'. This legend, passed from generation to generation in the village, was told to the children on a day that we went out of the setting and we found the ruins of an old fountain. According to the people in the village, a princess was locked inside the fountain by the king because she refused to marry her promised groom. Since then the fountain became enchanted and on the night of the full moon it is possible to hear the princess singing (the old fountain appears in Figure 5.16).

Figure 5.16 Memories and stories that pass through generations.

The children listened to the story in silence, becoming fascinated by the mystery of the legend. Through their reactions, I remembered my own childhood and the day my grandmother also told me this story.

Apart from the conversations and the many discoveries, the walks around the community and the days spent in the farm promoted a feeling of detachment from the rules and routines of day care, which allowed the children and adults to be freer to share experiences and feelings. In a way these times were similar to being on holiday or going on a visit far away, even though we were simply outside the setting in our own locality. Everyone at these times felt more relaxed, more spontaneous and able to delight in shared moments of fun such as running, laying down in the grass or racing with the wheelbarrow, as Figure 5.17 shows.

Another significant experience for strengthening bonds of companionship between adults and children was the one night camping in the farm with families and professionals. To celebrate the beginning of the year and our enthusiasm about outdoor play experiences, we challenged the parents to sleep for one night in tents and to share a meal around the fire with all the families from the group. Exceeding our expectations, the majority of parents fully engaged in this initiative, assuming an active role in the preparation and mobilising all the resources to guarantee that different planning details were considered (e.g. meals, places to accommodate everyone, light conditions, wood for the fire, barbecue structure). During the evening we all shared a hot meal and the time was marked by many conversations, laughs and songs around the fire. Children were very excited to be on the farm during the night and were happy to share that experience with the important adults in their lives (parents and professionals). The following morning, as we woke to the sounds of Nature and children giggling, we were surprised by a delicious breakfast prepared by the parents. Children could not have been happier to wake up next to their friends and their happiness was contagious. We spent the morning on the farm

Figure 5.17 During outdoor play children have the possibility to get to know adults in a different way.

and the children had the opportunity to show their parents what they most liked doing in that area (e.g. picking strawberries). After lunch everyone returned to their homes, grateful for the experience (Figures 5.18a–c show some of the captured moments). Camping in the farm was an important contribution to the development of strong relationships with the families. It created the time and space for families and professionals to get to know and trust each other.

With the camping happening at the beginning of the year, it was a way to prepare and engage the families in the outdoor experiences that would come after. A few months later we made another proposal to the families, suggesting a sleepover with the children in the setting, but this time without the parents. Despite being the first time that many children had spent any night away from their families, all parents responded positively and commended our initiative.

As with the camping activity, spending a night out, just professionals and children, was a marvellous experience that allowed us to interact in a very special way. Having the entire building to ourselves, to see everyone in their pyjamas and to play in the dark with flashlights, was something experienced with great enthusiasm by all. In the outdoors, children had the opportunity to observe the sunset, the stars and the full moon, something that they rarely did at home.

Regardless of the children's age and the fact they were away from their parents, the night was calm, with many fun and magical moments. When exhaustion finally took over, the children fell asleep and they only woke when the parents started to arrive in the morning to share breakfast with us. Some parents were astonished when we told them that the children did not cry or ask for them during the night. During breakfast everyone was in a good mood and it was possible to sense an atmosphere of joy and closeness of children, families and professionals. Figure 5.19 is a picture of the group.

Figures 5.18a Families setting up the tent for the night.

Figure 5.18b Preparing a nice barbecue for dinner.

Figure 5.18c A joint picnic in the farm the following morning.

Figure 5.19 A moment to remember – the first time that many of the children had spent a night away from their parents.

Myths about under threes

Young children cannot focus on the same activity for a long period of time

As we get older, we develop different interests and skills that allow us to stay focused for longer periods of time. However, it is not correct to assume that young children are not capable of investing in one activity for a long period of time, since the investment that he or she will dedicate to the activity is intrinsically dependent on the level of initial stimulation and thereby motivation and the level of stimulation created by the action itself.

According to Portugal and Laevers (2010), children's involvement in an activity is an important factor in evaluating the quality of the educational environment. If the opportunities offered to the child reflect their interests, if the adult is responsive and caring and if other basic needs are fulfilled, we may assume that these are good conditions to achieve high levels of involvement. Involvement is characterised by concentration, persistence, satisfaction, energy, precision and creativity, being understood as a continuum that goes from no activity to an experience that is extremely intense (Portugal & Laevers 2010). In a high level of involvement, children are totally immersed in the task and distractions hardly affect the activity (see Chapter 6 for a more detailed explanation about involvement). In these situations it is possible to assume that children perform in Vygotsky's zone of proximal development (Vygotksy 1978) since the activity is complex and challenging enough for the child to overcome personal barriers.

In the outdoors, the multitude of stimuli available to the children allows them to find different interests, creating good opportunities for high levels of involvement. However, in order to guarantee that children do become involved in their play it is important to make sure that they have the time and the support for it. Quick visits to the setting's outdoor area, just to allow children to stretch their legs, will not allow for a deep investment in the activity and therefore deep learning. Children need time and space to experiment, to fail, to try different strategies and approaches, and it is not possible to do that in ten minutes of recess time.

Young children are not capable of playing with each other cooperatively because they will easily enter into conflicts

The egocentrism of young children evolves in a positive way, if good conditions of interaction among peers are created. It is important for children to learn how to be with others, acquiring knowledge and skills to become social individuals, able to interact, understand and empathise with others.

In the outdoors, children can choose those moments to communicate and play with others, since the characteristics of the space allow for a more relaxed interaction.

Additionally, since the adult is not able to be everywhere at the same time, children have the opportunity to learn by themselves and learn to manage conflicts or overcome other problems. In this way, it is important the adult avoids intervening when it is not absolutely necessary, giving the children the opportunity to negotiate and to establish their own social rules and to discover they can solve their problems (Broadhead & Burt 2012). The adults can still be close by, and can be watching without interrupting just in case they feel they might be needed.

With time, children enjoy the company of other children and a sense of companionship starts to emerge. Conflict will always be present in the interactions of children, but that does not mean that they cannot develop attitudes of cooperation, respect and friendship.

6 Adults thinking about children

Figure 6.0 Adults have the responsibility to expand children's horizons.

Summary

What we achieve with children is for the most part down to the adults:

- their attitude to children;
- their approach with children;
- their understanding of and security with child development;
- and their knowledge and understanding of the processes of teaching and learning.

This is probably even more so in an environment such as the outdoors, which is not what most people would envision as a teaching environment. This is usually viewed as a space inside with seating and tables. Outside might have seating but it would not be the main item. An outside teaching environment would include elements like the weather and natural resources, such as soil, plants and animals. There might be equipment and resources outside and these could be man-made or purchased. But it does not have the formality of most indoor teaching spaces and so people may not know how to behave in that space. Therefore, it is incredibly important to help staff fully understand why the environment outside is so significant and how to use and take most advantage of that environment.

With this in mind we decided to take you through the process of one person, from not knowing a huge amount about working outside in a teaching and learning environment, to fully understanding and loving working outside with young children. We hope that in this way you can come to appreciate that it is possible with knowledge, skills and patience to create your own outdoor space for children. You will come to see that the outdoors is not a frightening place or a place where learning cannot occur, but rather the exact opposite.

An interview with Gi

So, we will take you through the story of Gi (the teacher in this book, shown in Figure 6.1) telling in her own words how she came to spend most of her day outside exploring with young children, helping them to learn and develop.

Figure 6.1 Gi (Gisela Dias) – the early childhood teacher of the children and co-author of this book.

Why did you start this project?

I can say my connection with the outdoors and Nature has been a part of me since I can remember. My parents are unconditional lovers of the outdoors, and so the outdoors was a place that was well known to us from the beginning and I was always inspired by it from a very early age. When I was only four months old I went camping for the first time and I have never stopped since then. My childhood memories are filled with long walks in the countryside, joyful picnics and relaxing naps in a blanket in the shadow of a tree (see Figures 6.2a–b for examples of childhood memories). I remember with nostalgia the time when I went looking for chameleons with my father. We spent a lot of time trying to find the chameleon and when we finally did, it was my father who placed him on our clothes to show how he could change colour. It was an amazing transformation. Afterwards, we released the animal back into Nature, as my father and mother firmly believed in the moral values such as respect and kindness towards others (people, animals or plants) and they never missed an opportunity to teach us such values.

Figures 6.2a–b The influence of childhood experiences in the love for the outdoors. Young Gi having a shower surrounded by Nature and with her family on a picnic.

Without a doubt, I can say that my childhood experiences had a great influence in my decision to embrace this early years outdoor project. Despite this, what triggered the change was the in-service training course about outdoor learning in the early years. The course was promoted by the board of the setting where I worked, since they always believed in the importance of the natural world, and the fact that the natural world needs to be valued and protected. The board of the setting gave great encouragement and support for the development of outdoor practices and the in-service course was a turning point in the way I understood outdoor play. Going beyond a theoretical approach, the training course prompted me and the team to reflect, discuss and question deep-rooted practices. Throughout the course I started to observe children in a different way, thinking deeply about which activities would respond to their needs and interests. I was challenged by something new and I felt a very strong desire to take risks and step outside my comfort zone.

However, it is important to recognise that my involvement in outdoor play did not happen suddenly. My adventures outside occurred gradually, in a planned and reflective way, with the collaboration of my team and the children's families. Every day we were outside, I recognised that I and the children felt better there, always finding opportunities and challenges for learning. Figures 6.3a–b exemplify those unexpected moments of discovery. As children explored the outdoors, they asked many questions and I realised how much I did not know about Nature. This project made me understand that we have to constantly be curious about the world around us, acquiring new information, eager to learn alongside the children, so that we can instil the interest, knowledge and understanding in the young. In this way we progressively become better professionals. I like to think that in life, as in Nature, we always have the opportunity to renew ourselves.

Figure 6.3a How intriguing and beautiful can a spider web be?

Figure 6.3b There is always something new to discover where we least expect it.

Points to note when embarking on such a project

In summary, when thinking about setting up an outdoor project for the youngest child:

- Get inspired about the outdoors through reading or going on courses.
- Be prepared to give yourself time to get to know your outdoor space.
- Learn more about the natural world through books and the Internet.
- If you were not brought up having the outdoors as part of your life, start now. Buy the right clothing – waterproof trousers and coat, Wellington boots, gloves, hat and scarf and for the summer a long sleeved tee-shirt and a hat.
- Get outside, whatever the weather.

Research evidence

We are so lucky in the twenty-first century as we have such ease of access to so much knowledge. For example, the Woodland Trust has a Nature calendar, to help you keep an eye out for seasonal events within the natural world; they have a 'things to do in the woods' section. If you look at the BBC website it has a section on British wildlife and a

Nature wildlife site – both are full of really useful information (see Chapter 7 for a list of resources). Simply taking an identification book with you when you go out can be a fantastic teaching opportunity as you and the children together try to identify something.

The right clothing is essential, and can be the difference between enjoying and not enjoying being outside. A project in a school in Oxfordshire found that by going out every week, dressed in clothing to fit the weather conditions, children were happy and able outside and were fine staying out for up to an hour, even if it was cold and wet for the entire time (Bilton & Crook 2016). One of the support staff in this book hated going outside but through this project and having the right clothing found she now embraces the outside and loves it!

Is there any theoretical framework that inspires and guides your action?

I do not follow a specific theoretical approach or model. The experience accumulated over the years in day care allowed me to choose principles and theoretical orientations that best suit my style. I do, however, embrace a set of principles that give meaning to my work in early childhood education:

● the child as active and competent;
● the need to respond well to every child;
● learning and development as interlinked and holistic processes.

Within these parameters I have to feel comfortable with my choices, believing in the support that they can give me to develop quality educational responses to children, their families and the community. I defend a flexible and questioning attitude towards education, in which practices and strategies can be adapted or transformed if they do not respond adequately to the daily needs in day care.

Indeed, the fact that there is no compulsory curriculum in early childhood education in Portugal (in particular from zero to three) gives me greater flexibility to develop my own way of doing things, inspired by different approaches and authors. Of course the setting is regularly evaluated by government services, but this should not stop innovation or a willingness to improve educational practices.

I highlight, for example, Experiential Education as a model that has had great influence on me, since I consider that well-being and involvement are basic concepts to guide and support educational intervention. In Figures 6.4a–b children's expression and posture show signs of happiness, openness to the world, energy (Figure 6.4a), concentration, persistence and endurance (Figure 6.4b), vital to learning and development. Also, inspired by the Experiential Education approach, the dimensions of sensitivity, autonomy and stimulation, linked to the adult style, help me to reflect and evaluate my own practice and to facilitate a process of continuing improvement.

In the daily interactions with children I feel that I have a role of learning facilitator. I do not see myself as a teacher that 'dumps' knowledge onto the children (recipients). When I accompany the children in their explorations I talk to them, ask questions or introduce materials, trying to give them an active and central role in the process of learning. For me it is an emotional experience and a pleasure to feel that we are learning together. With this in mind, I support freedom of choice, in the sense that the child has the possibility to choose what he/she wants to do and how, knowing that his/her decision will be respected. Figure 6.5

Figures 6.4a–b Quality educational practices promotes well-being and involvement.

Figure 6.5 In the greenhouse, children were playing on their own, without adult supervision. The photograph was taken without them noticing.

illustrates a situation when the children went to explore on their own and got out of the adult's sight. They were capable to manage risk and to interact peacefully with each other.

However, giving freedom to choose does not involve an attitude of permissiveness, as it is sometimes interpreted. Giving freedom to choose involves rules and limits, the promotion of an attitude of responsibility, autonomy, respect by others, commitment and dedication. This is a difficult task for the teacher and it has a great importance in the outdoor space, where the adult cannot (and should not) control everything.

I believe learning can only occur if the child feels safe, peaceful and happy, knowing that the significant figures trust and believe in their abilities. Carefully observing each child is crucial to knowing each boy or girl. I try to grasp their interests, seeking to stimulate learning by considering what seems to be most significant for them. From my perspective, the pedagogical relationship should be based on trust and affection, since learning cannot occur without these two dimensions. And these relationships also demand an attitude of openness and authenticity from the adult. We cannot establish a relationship with a child without showing ourselves and our world. For me, it is important that children know my family, what type of things I like or do not like, what makes me feel happy or sad. The process of sharing cannot happen in a unilateral way, in which only the adult has all the knowledge.

Besides a stable relationship with the adult, it is very important that the child feels part of the group. Aware of this, I work with the aim of promoting a good group atmosphere, where every child feels respected in his or her individual characteristics. I value diversity and I try to make children understand it is an enriching factor in their lives. I want children to feel unique but, at the same time, part of a plural and diverse group (family, community, country). Figure 6.6 shows a moment of help and empathy between children.

Figure 6.6 Respecting each other's strengths and weaknesses, the children developed a strong sense of friendship. The girl helps the boy to go up the hill, holding his arm and saying encouraging words.

Points to note when considering the theories behind the practice

In summary the teacher is:

- A learning facilitator, who is fully involved with the children and sees the relationship with them as paramount. Adults need to be open, authentic, trustworthy, affectionate; responding in a sensitive, stimulating and autonomous way.

And the basic principles for outdoors are:

- The child is viewed as active and competent.
- Each child needs to be responded to with sensitivity.
- Learning and development are interlinked and holistic processes.
- The mutual values are of promoting an attitude of responsibility, autonomy, respect for others, commitment and dedication.
- The action of the teacher includes talking to children, asking questions and introducing new materials.
- The children need to feel safe, happy, peaceful and part of a group, knowing that the significant figures trust and believe in their abilities.

Research evidence

The adults in a child's life need to have many attributes and the Effective Provision of Preschool Education (EPPE) research talks about 'quality' mattering. Quality consists of well qualified staff, who have 'warm interactive relationships with children', who see educational and social development as equally important, and these characteristics were found to ensure better progress and outcomes for children. In quality settings there was a belief that viewed teaching as a part of the role of working with young children; the job was not simply viewed as child care (Sylva, Melhuish, Sammons, Siraj-Blatchford & Taggart 2004, p. 1).

If we return to the work of Siegel (2012), shared in Chapter 1, he talks about the importance of relationships with children; again, this is supported by the work of Vygotsky (1978) and Laevers (1994). It is that closeness of the relationship that is so important in giving a strong grounding to a child. According to Laevers (2003), to promote an emancipated citizen, someone who is genuine, emotionally healthy, eager to explore and to interact with the surrounding world, it is crucial to adopt an experiential attitude. In this approach, the early childhood teacher should pay close attention to the needs and interests of the child, focusing on his or her inner experience. Furthermore, the early childhood teacher should be aware of his/her own experience as a way to better empathise and understand the child's perspective. The experiential attitude develops into three important dimensions that should guide and support the adult's intervention – sensitivity, autonomy and stimulation. Sensitivity is related to the importance of developing a deep and authentic relationship with children, making them feel listened to, understood and accepted. It involves paying attention to the behaviours and feelings of children, responding adequately to the needs of affection, support, physical contact, respect and safety (among others). A sensitive attitude is equally related to helping children accept and express their feelings, promoting self-knowledge and confidence to explore. Autonomy as a dimension of the adult's intervention is considered to be the creation of opportunities for the child to choose, experiment and have an active role in the environment. It is related to the participation of children in the mutual construction and definition of rules and limits, recognising the child as competent and responsible. Finally, stimulation is related to an attitude of expanding and enriching the opportunities that are presented to the child. The early childhood teacher should act as a facilitator in learning, introducing activities, information or materials, taking the greatest advantage of the children's interests and instigating curiosity and enthusiasm about discovering new things (Portugal & Laevers 2010).

The experiential attitude is intrinsically connected to a permanent investment in evaluation and reflection about quality educational practices. Following Laevers's (2003) perspective, well-being and involvement of children are the best indicators to access educational quality, since they express how the children's needs are being fulfilled (well-being) and how the opportunities offered in the environment can truly challenge, motivate and instigate children to act upon their interests. Emotional well-being can be described as feelings of pleasure, satisfaction, serenity and vitality, which allow us to be open, spontaneous and available to the world. In order to achieve emotional well-being, a group of basic needs (e.g. physical needs, affection, security, recognition) have to be assured, so the children can feel good about themselves, open to interactions, able to adapt to new situations and confident to face challenges. This mirrors Maslow's (2013) hierarchy of needs originally presented in the 1940s, in which he argues that children's basic needs – physiological and safety – must be met before all other needs can be. Likewise this is supported by the work of Bronfenbrenner (1979) who talks in terms of how everything in a child and his/her environments will impact how he/she grows and develops. According to Laevers, Moons and Declercq (2012, p. 6), 'our role is to offer the necessary emotional support and conditions for the child to learn to interact successfully with environment, people, places and objects and in doing so strengthen personal, social and emotional development'. Involvement is represented by the effect that the environmental conditions have on the child. It is a dynamic indicator expressed by elements such as concentration, persistence, motivation, energy, creativity and fascination. Involvement is a quality of human activity that results from the interaction of environment characteristics and child needs and interests. Following this line of thought, educational settings that promote challenges, instigating the child to mobilise his/her best capabilities and to perform at a high mental level, will create the appropriate conditions for learning to occur. Involvement is associated with a state of intrinsic motivation, in which the child is stimulated to explore areas of uncertainty, performing in a zone of proximal development (Laevers 1994; Vygotsky 1978). It is important to consider that 'involvement is different from the "fun" a child can experience during an activity and is not the result of sheer "entertainment". Consequently, with involvement we are far away from superficial learning' (Laevers, Moons & Declercq 2012, p. 12). Well-being and involvement are closely connected, since it is very unlikely for a child to achieve high levels of involvement if his or her basic needs are not fulfilled and well-being alone is not a sufficient condition for learning and development to occur.

When you first started this project what were your main concerns?

When this project started the children were between 14 and 18 months old. They were often seen as babies, and this brought many fears and concerns. The dimensions and layout of the outdoor space was a big challenge for their age and level of autonomy. Faced with an outdoor area as vast and diverse as the one we had in the setting, I feared that a child would go out of my sight. In the beginning I did not feel prepared to deal with accidents that could arise when children were alone, without an adult. I did not know how I would explain to the parents the fact that something negative had happened without me being nearby. Also, I was afraid that a child might leave the area of the setting, becoming exposed to other dangers in the street (e.g. cars, strangers).

But gradually I started to realise that my presence, by itself, was not a sufficient condition to prevent problems, since they could happen even if I was a metre away. The fear that a child could leave the setting's grounds also started to diminish, since the outdoor space was completely enclosed.

Apart from fears related to accidents, I was apprehensive of the possibility of children getting sick during the winter, especially after playing with water. To solve this situation it was very important to give children appropriate clothing (waterproof suits and rubber boots), which allowed them to play freely, without so many worries (Figures 6.7a–b show the waterproof suits and the warm clothes children wear during the winter). Parents' help was very important in this matter, since the equipment was bought by them. Over time, it was the parents themselves who reported the importance of going outside to actually prevent the children falling ill, considering that since the beginning of the project the children had fewer health problems. Besides regular colds and flu, some children had respiratory and skin problems, such as asthmatic bronchitis and eczema. It is important to mention that we always encouraged the parents to talk to the children's paediatrician about the implications of playing outside, especially when they were in a more fragile condition (e.g. periods of asthma crisis). We wanted the parents to realise that we were concerned and did not want to expose the children to situations that could jeopardise their health. We were open to working with other professionals, such as physicians, to create the best conditions for children to thrive. All paediatricians reacted very positively to letting the children play in the open air, considering that it would be very good for their health. The doctor's approval and praise strengthened the confidence of parents and made them more enthusiastic about outdoor play (even during the winter).

Figure 6.7a The waterproof clothes and rubber boots remained in the setting (each child had their own). Appropriate equipment is essential to facilitate good experiences outside.

Figure 6.7b On a winter morning the children went for a walk in the community.

In general, I think that my fears started to disappear as the outdoor space became an increasingly familiar and comfortable context for myself and the children. We had not been used to being outside all the time and we had to learn how to enjoy and take the most from it. Children became increasingly agile and at ease in the outdoors and the adults also felt progressively more confident to take risks, based on the knowledge that was being acquired gradually. Consequently, it was important to reflect regularly, think and rethink the project over and over, ensuring we constantly relooked at the organisation of the adult and material resources, as well as time and space. Still, I believe that the close relationship I established with my team, in which I include families, my educational helper and Gabriela, was essential to overcoming the difficulties.

Points to note when considering your concerns about such a project

In summary when starting a project with young children you may feel:

- Apprehensive about the possibility of accidents, and parental concerns.
- Concerned that children will become more readily sick.

These anxieties are overcome by:

- Going out every day with the children.
- Really getting familiar with the environment and space.
- Giving children the right protective clothing.
- Realising that the experiences outside make the children more agile and therefore more resilient.
- Understanding that accidents can occur despite an adult being right next to the child.
- Understanding that children dressed appropriately do not get sick from being outside.
- Constantly reflecting upon the organisation of the adults and children, the use of time and space and the experiences the children are having.
- Talking to and involving the parents as you explore outdoors.

Research evidence

The environment for learning can often be overlooked when thinking about what impacts on the quality of education a child receives. There seems to be three components to the equation of education – the 'what', which is the curriculum, the 'who' being the child and their family and the 'how' being the environment (including the provision of resources, the layout of the space, the daily routines and within that of course the adult expectations) (Bilton 2010). The fact that the EPPE (IoE 2016) project used a grading scale of the environment to measure the quality of the education does indeed suggest it is important. Siraj-Blatchford, Sylva, Muttock, Gildren and Bell (2002) describe the environment for learning as the 'pedagogical framing', or the 'behind the scenes' (p. 8) work, to support teaching and children's learning. Both Bilton and Siraj-Blatchford argued that this 'pedagogical framing' has a strong bearing on the outcomes for children. So some of this behind the scenes work includes understanding the space you will want to use for education, knowing how much time to spend there, thinking about resources needed and accepting that we are human and mistakes will be made. As long as you understand that mistakes are fine, you can learn from them!

Turning to safety we need to appreciate that a child cannot be kept safe all the time and by wrapping a child up and not allowing them to test their judgements they will actually become extremely unsafe. If a child does not learn to know their own body limits, how can they face the many challenges including danger as they grow up? Risk is an important part of growing up and we know that children are increasingly being brought up in societies where risk aversion is becoming the norm (Gill 2007; Whitebread, Basilio, Kuvalja & Verma 2012). Getting the right balance between what is and what is not an acceptable risk is therefore incredibly important. To help you make these decisions, regular risk and risk benefit assessments of your outdoor environment are vital (see Chapter 4 for a detailed discussion about risk).

Finally, you do not catch an illness outside; you catch most diseases inside. Think of the common colds, coughs, gastric diseases, pneumonia, and more major diseases, such as tuberculosis (TB), dysentery, mumps, measles and so on; they are all caught and spread in overcrowded and badly ventilated environments. Following this line of thought, the Portuguese research project 'Environment and health in children day care centres' (ENVIRH) concluded that the facilities analysed had reduced or inadequate means of ventilation in the activity rooms. A high level of pollutants (e.g. carbon dioxide, fungi, bacteria) above the reference values were found in the air, which may facilitate the transmission of diseases and the aggravation of respiratory problems (Mendes *et al.* 2014).

Outside is full of fresh air and light – both are critical for good health. If children get chilled, they are highly likely to get ill (Johnson & Eccles 2005). Hence, we should ensure children are wrapped up in the right clothing to prevent illness. Rickets, the disease caused by lack of vitamin D, is on the increase in a number of countries and it is through sunlight that this vitamin is synthesised. Therefore, for many health reasons, children must get outside regularly.

How would you describe your relationship with the families? How did you enable the parents to be happy about their children exploring outdoors?

The success of the work in day care is based on forming, developing and keeping close and meaningful relationships with the families. Parents should be seen as partners, with whom it is important to create a spirit of cooperation and understanding. We need to work as a team, trying to create the best opportunities for the development and learning of children.

Therefore, I tried to involve the families in all stages of the project. Before we took any initiatives, we met with the parents to explain the project and its main goals. In the beginning and as we went along, we gave the parents space to share their opinions and we made ourselves available to talk to but also find strategies that pleased everyone. The parents had concerns, just like me. The project moved away from what we were used to doing, so it was important to create a positive atmosphere to aid the gradual transition to a different way of working.

When the project began I started to share with the parents what had happened in the outdoors, trying to reveal the main benefits of those experiences in terms of cognitive, social, emotional and physical development. Through informal talks at the end of the day, exchange of emails, messages in backpacks, sharing photos and videos, it was possible to create a very positive climate that made parents feel an important part of these experiences. Small gestures, such as sending an email with a set of photographs of the child, accompanied by a short description of the situation, helped to dissipate fears and to create bridges of communication between parents, child and teacher (see Figure 6.8). With the shared information, parents were able to understand the value of those experiences and to assign meaning to the children's reports. With ease we created a portfolio of each child's development, in which I and the parents wrote the main achievements and remarkable experiences during the year. It should be noted that often this work of recording and sharing information had to be done after working hours.

From: Gi
To: Parents
Subject: Dreamy butterflies
Dear all,
Yesterday we were able to experience something amazing with the children. We received two baby butterflies inside a cardboard box with colourful flowers and we went outside to free them into the natural world. It was a magical and exciting moment that inspired the children to ask a lot of questions – 'Will we teach the butterfly how to fly?'; 'Is she a baby?'; 'Where will she go?'

We compared the butterflies with the images in a book we have been reading and the children identified the species.

Outside we gently placed the butterflies in flowers and the children were able to observe them very closely. The butterflies stood still for a couple of minutes and when they started to fly everybody clapped with excitement and joy. What a beautiful moment!

Now you know more about your child's day, go talk to him/her about his/her adventures and enjoy the photos I have sent you in the attachment.
Gisela Dias

From: Gi
To: Parents
Subject: Prepared for the cold
Dear Parents,
Because we had a cold day, we decided to offer a different morning to the children. We went for a walk around the village, discovering the community. We went to the grocery shop and bought cookies, we talked to the children in the primary school and we said 'hello' to several people that came across our way. We even passed in front of the house of Diogo Cruz [one of the children]! In this way, we kept very warm, since we were in constant activity: running along the paths, climbing up trees, cuddling dogs, etc.

It was an amazing morning, in which we took advantage of the benefits of the outdoors.

In order to allow this type of experience to continue, it is important that the children come to the day care dressed in warm clothes and always carry a winter hat in their backpack.

So you can better understand our day, look at the photographs attached.
Best regards,
Gi

Message sent by a dad to the adults of the group:
The walks in the village nourish children's curiosity and sense of freedom. These experiences are a big asset, which will influence them in the future, I'm sure. In the present, outdoor play makes them happier and more curious children.
Please continue the good work, keeping awake the 'Tom Sawyer' that exists in them.
Be eternal dreamers. Be happy.
Thank you.

From: Gi
To: Leandro Family
Subject: Our boy
Hello Mum and Dad,
After our talk today, I have sent you some photographs of Leandro's day in the setting. I think that after seeing the photos you will believe me when I say that he eats fruit. Indeed, with regards to strawberries, the more, the better! He has been eating well. I think the outdoors increases his appetite!
Also, he has been surprising us outside. He is very persistent and adventurous. On the farm, where the ground is very uneven, he walks without asking for help, overcoming the obstacles that emerge in the way.
I have already realised that he feels more confident when he has full attention from the adult, so we will do our best to support him in this way.
Enjoy the photos and show them to him. I think he will enjoy them!
Love,
Gi

Figure 6.8 An exchange of messages (emails) between families and the early childhood teacher.

However, the benefits brought by this initiative were so many that this compensated for the extra time I spent doing so. What father or mother does not want to see their child happy? To receive a nice photograph in the mail box after a difficult day at work can do a lot for the well-being of the family.

In addition, parents were always invited to spend some time with the children outside, often being amazed at what the children knew and were able to do. Inside, we liked to share with the families the 'treasures' found by the children during the day (rocks, sticks, snails, shells, butterflies and so on).

The development of good lines of communication facilitated the solution of small problems that sometimes emerged. For example, in the beginning of the project we started to notice that some parents got upset when the children took dirty clothes home. After talking to the parents to understand their perspective and explain ours, we found shared solutions (e.g. dress the child in older clothes) that helped the parents recognise that dirtiness was a sign of a good day spent outside (see Figure 6.9)!

Also, at different stages of the project the parents' collaboration was essential. Apart from providing the appropriate clothes and footwear to play outside, they were always available to help us improve the space. With the families' contribution we repaired and created new structures outside and we renewed the materials available in areas such as the muddy space. The families were interested in participating in social activities, such as spending a night camping in the farm, as shown in Figure 6.10a. Those moments of sharing and interaction were marvellous and allowed us to get to know each other better. In the activities such as camping, families worked as a team and each contributed in their own way. A grandmother prepared a cake, a father carried the wood in his tractor to make a big fire, a group of parents prepared a warm soup for dinner, etc. (Figure 6.10b).

Figure 6.9 Enjoying playing with soil with no fears about dirtiness.

Figure 6.10a Families and professionals get together to spend a night camping in the farm. A marvellous gathering around the fire.

Figure 6.10b 'It's my dad's tractor!' Parents like to collaborate and children enjoy this and feel proud.

Finally, the parents' feedback about how the children felt with this project was extremely important, helping me to better plan and evaluate our actions and activities for the future.

Points to note when considering parents

In summary, to ensure parents feel happy with their children working outside:

- See them as equal partners and all as a team.
- Empathise with the parents, understand why they have anxieties.
- Meet with the parents regularly to let them know what is happening.
- Be clear about the aims and objectives of working outside and relay those to the parents.
- Let the parents share their views, be it concerns and anxieties or enthusiasm.
- Be willing to compromise and make adjustments in the light of parental ideas.
- Keep in contact with parents through informal conversations at the end of the day, exchange of emails, messages in backpacks, sharing photos and videos. Send an email with a set of photographs of the child, accompanied by a short description of the situation.
- Get the parents to give feedback about their child's experiences and their views of the project generally.
- Invite parents to see the space in action.
- Invite parents to mend and make resources and equipment.

Research evidence

One cannot overstate the importance of the impact of the parents on the child's development, nor the importance of schools and staff being involved with the families. If we take the EPPE project findings for example, this demonstrates conclusively that where schools had very good links with parents, children were more successful (Department for Education 2004). The findings note that in schools that foster true partnership with parents, the learning experiences at school can be built upon back at home. It shows that: 'children who have a good home learning environment (HLE) and who attend a high quality pre-school, have better language development when they start primary school and make more progress than their peers over the primary school period' (Department for Education 2011, p. 4). It also demonstrates that where schools were involved closely with the parents: 'Disadvantaged boys were particularly helped by attending high quality pre-school: those from excellent pre-schools (in this small sub-sample) went on to succeed above expectation' (Department for Education 2011, p. 5).

How do you deal with accidents? How do you manage risk?

Initially, my ideas of trust, security and possibilities for children's autonomy were very limited. The level of challenge and risk in children's activities outside grew exponentially from the beginning of the project. Risk management, risk assessment and risk benefit demand that the teacher feels comfortable in the space, being able to encourage the child to explore and demonstrate confidence in their skills. In a scary moment, in which the child is testing their limits without knowing if he/she is going to succeed, it is important that they feel supported, regardless of the outcome. However, I recognise that it was not always easy to hide my fears when I saw a child climb a tree or play with tools. More often than not our desire to protect children comes across loud and clear, even though we have not said anything. Our feelings are transmitted through non-verbal cues and children are tuned in to pick these up. As I was aware of this situation, I tried to help the children to develop strategies for more easily dealing with risk. Through some questions or suggestions, it was possible to support children to overcome challenges, without making them feel devalued or incompetent ('Are you able to jump from there without help?', 'What do you think about asking Tomás to help you carry that log?').

The ability to manage risk is closely related to the relationship of trust developed with the families. Assuming that facing risks is very important for learning and development, it is important to explain to the parents how those situations are managed and promoted, guaranteeing that children are not exposed to dangers, hazards or extreme situations that they are not able to deal with. It is essential that parents find out and understand that dealing with risk is something that involves deep reflection, planning and evaluation from the teacher. I remember a situation, when we were planning to spend a day near a small stream, near the day care centre. Xavier (one of the boys from the group) told his mother that he needed to wear swimming shorts the next day, because we were going to the river. The following day, Xavier's mother arrived at the setting very worried and upset, because she felt that it was too dangerous to go to the river with two-year-old children who did not know how to swim. After talking to the mother and showing her some photographs of the place we were going to, she became more relaxed and relieved. She was able to see that the river was only a small stream where the water only reached up to the children's knees. This situation reinforced the need for constant dialogue with the families, to ensure that there was a strong understanding of what the teacher was doing and why.

Assuming that it is not possible, or desirable, to create risk free environments, it is vital to carefully prepare activities and know the places you are to visit. It may be necessary that the teacher goes to the outdoor area in advance, getting to know its main features. I often adopted this strategy when we left the setting to explore the community (e.g. a walk to the stream). This type of initiative demanded a previous plan, in order to choose the roads with less traffic and to avoid construction or farming areas, where the children were not able to freely walk (see Figure 6.11).

Figure 6.11 Going out of the setting does not need to be a stressful situation for the adult. It is important to plan in advance and to complete the necessary risk assessments.

Often, it was necessary to divide the group of children according to the goals of the activity or the number of adults available. If we had fewer staff it was important to ensure that safety was guaranteed and the logistics were covered (e.g. how many children would have to be changed after play and how many adults could help). A ratio of one adult to three/four children was considered prudent, so sometimes I went alone with a very small group of children. In this way more attention could be paid to the children. Within the larger group, it was difficult to keep track of everything that was happening and the more introverted children hardly got the support needed to face challenging situations. In a smaller group (three to four children) the adult was able to observe in a more systematic way and to promote risky play, assuring that safety conditions were present. Dividing the group created opportunities for closer interactions, which were important for children to feel cared for and supported. In this way, the division of the group did not occur in an arbitrary fashion. Children's need for risky play and the resources available were aspects that were taken into account.

Even with careful planning, it was not always possible to avoid accidents happening. Tears can represent moments of learning and it is important to help children deal with different emotions (see Figure 6.12). A bump on the head or a scratched knee are part of childhood and it can easily be explained to the parents if an honest and open attitude is adopted. The development of a good relationship with the families will facilitate the acceptance of these situations, recognising that accidents have a strong component of unpredictability and that they can happen in the day care centre or in the family environment.

Figure 6.12 Through errors, failures or accidents, learning occurs. Empathising and acknowledging children's emotions is crucial to help them overcome difficult situations.

Points to note when considering safety outside

In summary, when considering the safety side of outdoors, remember:

- The adult has to feel secure about the risks and challenges.
- Be aware that if the adult is scared about a situation a child is in, the non-verbal cues will be transmitted.
- When a child is in a risky situation ask them questions or make tentative suggestions to ensure they are thinking about what they are doing.
- Talk to the parents about the relevance of risk and challenge to young children and how tackling risk will make them safer in the long run.
- Make sure you know the area well that you are to visit, and therefore can demonstrate you have considered carefully the risks and possible issues.
- Encourage parents to understand that accidents happen and need to be seen as a learning experience.

Research evidence

See Chapter 4 for a detailed discussion about risk.

How did you improve your work – day in, day out?

Recognising that the early childhood teacher plays a key role in the process of learning and development in the outdoors, I think that it is essential to have an open and reflective mind, eager to change and improve. In this project we sought to create a dynamic of reflection and evaluation among the adults who accompanied the group of children, through regular meetings, shared records and informal conversations.

With the goal of monitoring the experiences in the outdoors in a rigorous way, we created a record keeping system (with written notes), based on the observations of children's play and which we completed daily. After the period spent outside, we recorded the most significant experiences, the main interests of the children and aspects of their play to improve and develop. The data collected was shared among the team, promoting a reflective approach that enabled us to consider the next steps or educational goals for the children and the style of the adult intervention.

In order to evaluate the project overall, we got together once a week, to discuss and analyse the process. In these meetings, apart from identifying the main benefits for children and aspects that we would need to improve, there was also a concern to understand how each team member felt in the outdoors. In this way, we tried to find solutions related to the management of the time, space, material and human resources that best responded to the identified needs.

It was very gratifying to recognise that as time passed adults found they had fewer and fewer difficulties and became more relaxed about working outside with such young children. The best indicator of the success of the project was the high level of satisfaction and commitment of the children outside, which affected the adults' attitude, keeping them motivated and inspired. The adults found that they experienced the project in an intense and emotional way. Their joy and enthusiasm was evident in the relaxed, pleasant and engaged attitude they adopted during children's play, which had not been apparent at the beginning of the project. It became natural to see adults run through the fields, paddling in the river and lying on the grass with the children. When we analysed those moments, the shared joy was identified as the best thing of the day. In Figures 6.13a–c moments of quality adult and child interaction are represented.

Figures 6.13a–c When adults are committed to children and outdoor play the experiences are enhanced. Outside, we can be truly available for children.

I would like to stress the importance of collaboration, mutual help and complicity among the adults in the pursuit of a project of this nature. Openness to change, flexibility and an innovative spirit from all adults were key dimensions for the success of the project.

Above all I feel that my role as an educator is to provide meaningful experiences in the child's life. If the time during day care is marked by strong and secure relationships and rich and diverse experiences are provided, we have built the essential pillars for future learning and development.

Points to note when considering the adult's role

In summary, to ensure outdoor education is successful for all:

- Be open, flexible and innovative in your thinking.
- Give the project time – the more confident the children become, the more the adults will become secure and calm.
- Have regular meetings, informal conversations and share records and notes.
- Create a record keeping system to monitor significant experiences, the main interests of the children and aspects of their play to improve and develop.
- Share the information with all staff to plan the next steps or educational goals for the children and the style of the adult intervention.
- Meet once a week to discuss the project – benefits to children in being outside, improvements to be made – and explore the viewpoints of the adults when outside to accommodate their concerns.

Research evidence

Making changes requires altering our mindset and generally having a flexible approach. Rose and Rogers (2012, p. 3) describe seven dimensions to the adult role when working with young children:

- the critical reflector
- the carer
- the communicator
- the facilitator
- the observer
- the assessor
- the creator.

What this means in practice is two things. Firstly, the adult working with young children has many roles to consider, which are integrative, and each contributes to the other. Secondly, in this approach one needs to consider not just what one does but rather who one is. If we only consider teaching from the angle of what we do, it does not enable us to consider why we do what we do. The why will evoke consideration and possible change. The critical reflector means that we will consider 'socially just practice' (p. 14) for example, because we will constantly be considering what is right for all, not just some children. Schon (1987) considers that reflection is not something that happens after an event, but also occurs during an event. Schon describes this as 'reflection on action' and 'reflection in action'. This is a process not an event. Being a critical reflector therefore is about a continuous process of finding out about children and developing an ever deeper understanding: 'I think that it is essential to have an open and reflective mind, eager to change and improve' (Gi).

7 Resources and facilities

Figure 7.0 Discovering multiple opportunities for learning outside through careful planning of the space.

Summary

To create good opportunities for learning and development outside it is important to carefully plan and organise the space. Thinking about which type of materials and structures can best respond to children's needs and interests and also identify the best strategies related to maintenance, storage and preservation of the play environment is a never-ending challenge for professionals. In this chapter we want to share our experiences concerning resources and facilities, explaining how we managed to progressively improve the outdoor space, without spending a great amount of money and by getting the families and the community on board as key partners in achieving the project goals.

Planning the outdoor space – key points

Dynamics of the environment

Planning for outdoor play demands a flexible attitude and an effort to take advantage of the special characteristics of the space – fresh air, open spaces, freedom of movements, natural elements. During outdoor play different opportunities for learning and development emerge, since the environment is constantly changing, offering new stimuli and challenges (e.g. weather changes, children's actions). This changing dynamic should be acknowledged in the outdoor provision and design. Critically one needs to be prepared for the impact that different weather conditions have on:

- resources (e.g. corrosion, wear and tear, instability, equipment that can become distorted with age and temperature);
- the site (an area might become too muddy for instance);
- play stimulus (e.g. fallen leaves on the ground, puddles of mud, which create opportunities for learning).

Therefore, one further has to consider the need to change or introduce new structures or objects as they become inadequate or children and staff lose interest in them. Once children explore the outdoors their interests evolve and spaces are explored differently, so it is necessary to keep adding or transforming the features of the space to guarantee its interest and attractiveness (see Figure 7.1 for an example of how to introduce different stimuli for the exploration of sand).

Figure 7.1 Who would have guessed that with a tin and sand it would be possible to draw?

The dynamic of the environment is also related to the singularity of each setting, group of children and professionals. Although we find it important to share our experiences and knowledge regarding outdoor play, and indeed there are many aspects of good practice to be followed, there also has to be a level of flexibility so that your own context with regard to the environment and the group of children can be accommodated. Space features and users' needs and interests are interrelated and have a great influence on how the space can be planned.

Sustainability

The maintenance of the outdoor environment is a very demanding task, so it is important to develop strategies to guarantee a sense of harmony and organisation in the space. A good storage system is essential along with a concern about the type of objects that are available. Natural materials should always be the first choice and small and fragile plastic objects should be avoided (e.g. Lego pieces). To enable children to experiment with water, the introduction of a tank to collect the rain is a good option to save money and protect the environment. In our case, we introduced a 1000 litre water tank, with a tap located at children's level so they could freely and easily collect the water (represented in Figures 7.2a–b).

Also, sustainability or endurance is related to the unique opportunities that can happen outside. For example, exploring large objects, making loud noises and playing with mud or other natural elements are activities that are not sustainable in the indoor environment. Being aware of the unique features of the outdoors means one can plan accordingly. To illustrate this point think about how different the activity represented in Figure 7.3 would have been if it had happened inside. It is most likely the children would have not been able to explore and play with the water as freely and spontaneously as they did in the outdoors.

Figures 7.2a–b The water tank promoted autonomy and self-regulation in children's play.

Figure 7.3 The outdoor provision cannot be a replica of the indoors. Children enjoyed the water play through the exploration of different types of objects.

Inclusion

The outdoor environment should be an inviting and comfortable space for all children and adults. It needs to provide stimulus and opportunities for children with differing needs and interests, acknowledging that each child is unique, with a particular learning rhythm. Having different types of activities and challenges caters for the different characters and their social, cognitive, emotional and physical development. Children should have the possibility to choose what they want to do and how, in a well thought out environment, where there are not too many choices to confuse them, or too few to leave them with no options. As Figure 7.4 shows, children are dispersed throughout the space according to their interests. From the adult's perspective it is important that professionals feel good outside, having the necessary conditions to support children's play.

Participation

A good environment for outdoor learning demands the participation of children, professionals, families and community members. As main users of the space, children's views need to be considered in the planning process. Their voices should be respected and valued, since they often see things differently from the adults. Likewise, the professionals' input is fundamental to guarantee that aspects concerning the logistics, safety and comfort are assured. Professionals need to adopt an attitude of constant reflection and assessment of the outdoor space, in order to understand how the environment is responding to children's interests and what can be done to improve it. In addition to the adults that directly accompany the children, other professionals from the setting can provide crucial support. For example, the kitchen and maintenance staff can help to solve the logistics that facilitate outdoor activity, like preparing simple meals for picnics or cleaning

Figure 7.4 Acknowledging children's exploratory impetus and curiosity is a key dimension in supporting quality play experiences outside.

the dirt that goes inside with children's clothes and boots (in Figure 7.5 children enjoy an afternoon snack near a stream after a walk in the community). Families and community members are other key partners in creating good opportunities for outdoor learning. If families and community members feel welcome and valued in the setting, they will easily help in several tasks, such as collecting everyday objects for play or putting their skills into action to construct/improve structures or materials to better equip the outdoor area.

Time

It is fundamental to distinguish the concept of outdoor play, as a way to learn and develop, from what is regularly understood as recess time, in which children are allowed to play on their own for a short period of time (15 to 30 minutes), enjoying a break from structured and directed activities. In order to truly profit from what the outdoors can offer, children need time – time to invest, time to explore, time to experiment, following their own pattern and reacting to the stimulus provided by the environment. Adults need to acknowledge the importance of time, making sure that children have the necessary conditions to achieve high levels of involvement and well-being. Equally, time for planning and reflection between professionals is tremendously important to guarantee quality outdoor play provision. Professionals need to talk to each other, share ideas, concerns and doubts without having the children around, asking for their attention. From our experience, we acknowledge that it is not always easy to find the time and the space to think and plan as a team. However, all this effort is highly rewarded when we observe children's happiness in the outdoors. Often, we took advantage of the children's nap time to evaluate what had happened during the previous days and to discuss each child's interests, achievements or difficulties, so we could outline our future actions.

Figure 7.5 With some sandwiches and cartons of milk/yogurt a picnic outside is easily prepared.

Overall, planning the outdoor space for children is a never-ending challenge, in which problems or obstacles must be seen as part of the process and as opportunities for improvement. The outdoor space should be planned with the same attention and concern given to the indoor environment, recognising that outside well-being and learning emerge.

Resources for playing, exploration and discovery

Providing interesting resources for outdoors demands careful attention to and reflection on children's behaviour. Through paying attention to the children's actions and initiatives, it is possible to retain important information that will help to decide what can be relevant and appropriate to introduce in the outdoor area to enrich play activities. For example, children's interest in collecting and transporting all sorts of things in the outdoor area was identified as a dimension that was not being adequately satisfied by the materials available. As children explore the outdoor environment, simple findings, like a feather, a shiny pebble or a minibeast are interpreted as important treasures that must be kept. In this case, we decided to introduce new objects, such as baskets, cloth bags and trolleys, so children could transport and keep what they wanted (see Figures 7.6a–c).

Another situation was related to the introduction of a greater variety of objects to use with water to create new opportunities for exploration. Apart from the different sized pots, pans and plastic containers, we introduced sprayers, soap dispensers, droppers and

Figures 7.6a–c Children greatly enjoy carrying things from one place to another. It is a way for them to feel competent, to have an effect on the environment and to gain a greater knowledge about the world.

syringes and it was fascinating to observe how captivating and challenging they were for children. As Figures 7.7a–c show, the use of the soap dispensers, syringes or sprayers demanded a certain practice of fine motor skills, in order to be able to get the water in and out, and it promoted social and creative behaviours, as children imagined stories and attributed meaning to the objects.

Figures 7.7a–c Providing interesting materials for children to play with demands an on-going creative effort from the professionals.

We present below a set of important ideas to have in mind when choosing resources for outdoor learning. Acknowledging that many more could be mentioned, these were the main themes that emerged as we observed and played with the children outside.

- Resources should be accessible for children to use freely. As children engage in outdoor play it is important for them to get inspired and stimulated by the different options available and this is not possible if everything is kept away and children have to ask for it every time they want to use something.
- The different objects available should be easy for children to carry. They cannot be too heavy or too big, thereby rendering them inaccessible.
- Materials should be provided in quantity and quality. It is important to guarantee a sufficient number of things to avoid disputes among children. Different type and size resources can promote 'big ideas' (e.g. construction of a hiding place) and challenges. (Figures 7.8a–b show how learning can occur through experimentation with different objects – a small container can be easier to carry but more difficult to fill if it has a narrow neck; transporting a big container full of water demands cooperation among children.)

Figures 7.8a–b Finding a balance between the quantity and quality of the materials provided.

- Children should be allowed to use objects and materials in different ways (e.g. to dig, to carry, to fill). Through creativity and imagination, they often give new purposes and meanings to things. In Figure 7.9a children improvised a bed for the baby using a cardboard box and old sheets and in Figure 7.9b the boy is sawing with two pieces of wood.
- Resources for outdoor play do not need to be expensive or elaborate. Open-ended materials offer rich opportunities for play and they tend to be more interesting for children than plastic toys. Most of the resources that we introduced in the outdoor

Figures 7.9a–b Open-ended resources introduce complexity in play, offering different action possibilities.

area can be found in any home, so they are easy to replace when needed (for examples see Figures 7.10a–b). Do remember that objects in the outdoors do not tend to last long and children should be allowed to play with them freely, without feeling pressurised to preserve or avoid damaging them.

Figures 7.10a–b   Old kitchen supplies can be very interesting for children, since they allow them to reproduce familiar experiences.

Here is a list of the different types of resources provided. Their role in children's exploring is represented in Figures 7.11a–h.

- Different-size bottles of shampoo or detergent
- Different-size plastic containers (preferably with the lid)
- Different-size bowls
- Different-size cans
- Sprayers
- Soap dispensers
- Spoons, pans and other kitchen utensils
- Sponges
- Droppers
- Syringes
- Gardening tools
- Wooden spatulas
- Styrofoam objects
- Golf tees
- Tweezers
- Magnifying glasses
- Different-size cardboard boxes
- Different-size baskets or cloth bags
- Egg cartons or sweet boxes (with several partitions)
- Tyres
- Different types of fabric
- Tubes

Figures 7.11a–h
These play resources do not normally appear in educational catalogues.

Note: When using bottles of cleaning or hygiene products make sure they are empty and remove the labels. Acknowledging that most of those products are toxic, it is important to make a clear distinction in the type of objects that can be used for play, removing names, brands, etc.

Fixed structures as areas for socialisation and physical challenges

Outdoor play is often seen as a moment for children to expend some energy and stretch their legs and there is no concern in relation to planning or resource provision. In this scenario, fixed and traditional structures (e.g. slides, swings, climbing apparatus) are frequently the only stimulus children have outside, offering poor opportunities for play. Furthermore, the possibilities offered by these fixed structures, quickly become less and less as the children get too familiar with them.

With these thoughts foremost in our minds, when we did decide to introduce fixed structures in the outdoor area we thought about them carefully, trying to consider and foresee the possible implications for children's play.

Here is a list of the main structures that were introduced in the outdoor area and some of them are represented in Figures 7.12a–e:

- Tree houses
- Tents
- Wooden tractor
- Tyre wall
- Hill with tunnels underneath
- Ramp
- Tyre swings
- Hanging ropes
- Musical board.

Apart from offering physical challenges, these fixed structures contribute to social interaction, cooperation, pretend play, etc., as the experiences reported in this book show.

The fixed structures served as a motive to involve families in the project, since their construction depended a lot on the parents' help and contribution. With the goal of building a tree house or a ramp for the sake of the children, parents and professionals worked side by side, developing and strengthening a cooperative and trusting relationship. In Figures 7.13a–b the inventiveness of the parents is represented as they built a wooden tractor for children to play with.

Community members also contributed to improve the outdoor space, offering construction materials, time and skills to help build some of the structures (e.g. tyre wall and hill) (in Figure 7.14 the construction of the hill is documented).

Storage, transport and comfort

As we mentioned above, sustainability is a key dimension of outdoor exploration that must be assured.

Regarding storage and transport, it is essential to have in mind that the outdoor area will never be a very tidy and clean space; otherwise, it means that it is not used by children. Materials tend to move around a lot, according to different activities and interests. However, this does not mean there should not be a proper storage system, which can promote some degree of orderliness to the space. Assuming that children's involvement in play is strongly dependent on the way the area is organised and how the resources are provided, it is understandable that a chaotic environment will not provide for the best conditions to outdoor exploration. From this perspective, there should be a concern to constantly check and confirm the condition of the materials and structures available,

Figure 7.12a–e
Fixed structures need to be well thought out so they can respond to children's interests (e.g. secluded places, physical challenges and pretend play).

Figures 7.13a–b Families and professionals got together during the weekend to improve the outdoor area. Many talents and skills were discovered.

Figure 7.14 The hill was built with the help of workers from the parish council, who offered their time and resources without any cost to the setting.

removing broken or unused things, which simply create a messy and uncared space that might also compromise children's safety.

In our experience, the storage system should be simple, making it possible to involve the children in the tidying process and to access the materials as they want. For example, hanging strong bags on the walls, pierced underneath to let the water out, was one of things we did to store different objects and avoid them being scattered everywhere (see Figure 7.15).

Moreover, we asked the local supermarket to give us two shopping carts to facilitate the transport of resources. The shopping carts and a large trolley were also useful to carry the younger children in when we went for long walks (see Figures 7.16a–b).

Concerning comfort, we were able to create the necessary conditions to have meals in the outdoor area, thanks to the help of the father of one of the children who built a table and benches suitable for the whole group (represented here in Figure 7.17a). The meals outside offered wonderful moments of connectedness between children and adults. They allowed us to avoid the intense noise of the dinner hall and enjoy each other's company in a calmer environment. Around the table many conversations and moments of closeness emerged, creating a strong sense of group identity. In Figure 7.17b, during the afternoon snack, one of the professionals decided to 'raise a toast' with two boys, in order to spur one of them, who did not like fruit, to drink the fresh orange juice. This was a clever strategy to promote good feeding habits, taking advantage of social interaction and reducing the pressure associated with forcing children to eat.

Furthermore, comfort in the outdoor area strongly depends on having the right equipment according to the weather conditions and activities. Dependent on the season, we made sure children had the appropriate clothing, always counting on the vital involvement and help of families (as is also mentioned in Chapter 6 and represented here in Figure 7.18).

Figure 7.15 Children must understand and use the storage system, taking an active role in looking after the environment.

Figure 7.16a–b Resources for transportation avoid unnecessary physical effort from adults. The outdoor play environment is only good for children if it provides the necessary conditions for adults to engage and support children's play.

Figures 7.17a–b Creating a family environment during meal time.

Figure 7.18 The right equipment promotes comfort during play.

The relationship between the indoor and outdoor environments

The outdoor and the indoor areas should be planned as a continuum, without aiming to replicate features or opportunities. If we recognise that human development occurs through different experiences that influence the way children understand and act on their environment, we must value and integrate the indoors and outdoors, assuming that both contribute to learning and growth. Following this line of thought, children need to feel a sense a continuity between spaces, understanding which type of behaviours or activities are more appropriate and supported in each respective area. Despite the different characteristics of the environments, adults should convey a coherent attitude, assuring children they can rely on and feel safe with them.

To promote a connection between the indoor and outdoor areas different strategies can be developed. It was noticeable that the impact and meaning of the experiences outside were so strong for children and adults that it had a great influence on the indoor environment, affecting the type of materials available, the conversations and the interests of the children. The group was allowed to move objects between spaces, but it was interesting to note that it was more frequent for them to carry things from the outdoor area to the classroom than the opposite (see Figure 7.19a). Often, children wanted to take a flower, a feather, a bird's nest or even a simple stick inside, so they could play with them once they returned from outside, show them to their parents or just keep them for the pleasure of collecting. Following this interest, we started to create a museum to display the different things brought from the garden, as a way to value what the children found and to emphasise experiences that were meaningful for the group (see Figure 7.19b). Moreover many photographs of outdoor exploration were exhibited and the children deeply enjoyed looking at them and carrying them around to show to their friends and families (see Figure 7.19c). Because it was not possible to print all the good photographs, we used the LED screen that we had to improvise photo/film sessions. Apart from the photographs and the natural elements brought by the children, folders of images about the natural world were created and available, in order to stimulate children's curiosity and language. These strategies, among others, allowed the group to remember the outdoor play experiences, revisiting the information and the feelings engendered by those memories. Likewise, it was a way to promote dialogue between children, professionals and families.

Additionally, different play resources were introduced in the indoor environment to create a connection between children's inventiveness outside. For example, to support and stimulate the interest in minibeasts and other animals, we provided small plastic animals that were very engaging for the children (see Figure 7.19d).

Figure 7.19a Playing with natural materials brought in from outside.

Figure 7.19b Preserving important memories with a museum of outdoor play.

Figure 7.19c Sometimes a picture is worth a thousand words.

Figure 7.19d Acting according to children's interests.

Loose parts and open-ended materials were available in the room, acknowledging their positive effects on children's play. In Figures 7.20a–c some examples of natural materials and loose parts available in the classroom are shown.

Figures 7.20a–c The importance and meaning of outdoor play experiences were expressed through the strong presence of natural elements in the activity room.

Other spaces and resources

The outdoor space of the setting where this project took place was large. We recognise that not all outdoor spaces are like that and professionals struggle to find the conditions to promote outdoor activity. However, although we started with a large space it was not well resourced and used. We had to work hard to create an inspiring environment. Equally, having a good outdoor area did not stop us from visiting other spaces in the community, taking advantage of the surrounding environment to enlarge children's experiences. We were surprised to find out how many interesting places existed near the setting that promoted several opportunities for learning and exploration (such as the small stream, in Figure 7.21, where children were able to interact with Nature in a very special way).

Figure 7.21 Finding other spaces outside the setting to enhance children's experiences.

Going out in the community demands meticulous and responsible planning – consideration of transportation, provision for basic needs, first aid measures, hygiene and comfort, among others. Taking plenty of time to plan, and trying to foresee and be prepared for the unexpected, are key principles for ensuring that the visits in the community are good experiences for everyone involved. Simple safety measures must be assured; for example, a good adult-child ratio, visiting the space first without the children and getting familiar with the best route to get to the destination (e.g. avoiding areas with a lot of traffic). Also, like other experiences outside, it is important to make sure children have adequate clothes and, according to the distance, it can be useful to carry some food, water, wipes, diapers and a first aid kit. When we went out with the children for a long period of time (all day; morning or afternoon) we prepared each child's backpack with these basic supplies and sometimes we asked a parent or another professional to carry the backpacks by car to our destination (see Figure 7.22). The same strategy was adopted to deliver lunch and we always made sure children ate properly in order to recover energy spent during play (normally children had a two-course meal plus fruit). The help from the families and other staff members during these days away from the setting were vital since we always went on foot and we were very involved with the children.

Overall, to go out and enjoy the outdoor space of the community it is essential to be bold, responsible and a good team player. Proper planning and cooperation among adults is crucial, assuming that there is nothing wrong in asking others to help (families or colleagues). However, being prepared does not mean being inflexible or anxious if things do not go according to the plans. During outdoor exploration surprises emerge constantly, so an open and flexible attitude is essential. This reminds us of the day when the children spontaneously decided to greet and talk to an old man who was enjoying the shadow of a tree (as is represented in Figure 7.23) and when we were invited by the

Figure 7.22 Planning in advance is crucial when we go out with very young children.

Figure 7.23 It takes a whole village to raise a child (African proverb).

mother of one the children to have a snack in her garden. These simple and spontaneous experiences were very meaningful for the group and they only occurred because we took the risk of venturing out of the setting, aiming to involve the children in the daily lives of the local community.

Conclusion

By sharing our own experiences about outdoor play with under threes we aim to inspire other professionals to go out with their children and profit from the many learning and developmental opportunities that natural environments can offer.

Working with young children is not an easy job and in order to create an interesting environment outside it is necessary to devote a great amount of time, reflective thinking, thorough planning and strength to learn from the different trials and errors. Apart from the associated demands, it is incredibly rewarding to support and witness the development of a young child in the first months/years of life. Supporting under threes' development is not merely about changing diapers, feeding and keeping children safe. Although those things are important to guarantee well-being, working with under threes goes beyond that, being a period of life in which the type of relationships and experiences lived strongly influence future development. As professionals working in education it is our responsibility to promote interesting opportunities so that young children can develop a sense of pleasure in learning and discovering that will allow for the comprehension of more complex things in the future. Following the words of Rachel Carson (2012), in the first years of life it is important to create the best conditions for wonder, fascination and awe without having to focus on specific learning outcomes that children are not ready to absorb. Through meaningful life experiences, accompanied by supportive adults, the child progressively gains a greater knowledge about the world, others and him or herself, growing into a healthy, curious and enthusiastic citizen.

It is important to mention that if you want to develop an effective outdoor project there is no single path to follow. The cultural environment, the setting, the children, the families and the professionals have a big influence in defining the best strategies to follow and the success of the project depends on their involvement and motivation. With this thought in mind, you should not think that it is impossible or too difficult to develop outdoor practices in your own setting only because you do not have the necessary outdoor space conditions or because the families do not want the children to get dirt on their clothes. If you feel motivated to invest in this approach the best thing to do is to start with small goals, small changes, and progressively adjust the strategies to your reality and obstacles. In doing so, it is crucial to adopt an attitude of constant reflection and evaluation, accepting the fact that failures are part of the process and the most important thing is to learn from them. Pay close attention to children's play. They will help more than you can imagine and you will probably be surprised with what you can achieve in a short period of time (e.g. just going outside every day for a minimum of 40 minutes can produce changes in the children and in your attitude as a professional).

Through this book it was our goal to deconstruct some myths about the under threes. Despite their age, young children are incredibly skilful and fast learners and they tend to surprise us every day. Adults often underestimate children, assuming that they are not capable of doing or understanding certain things, which it is not true most of the time. Our protective and caring impetus towards our youngest should not prevent us from setting challenges and allowing them to face problems and deal with situations of disappointment or success. Without being able to remember what it was like to be one, two or three years old, it is crucial to adopt an empathetic attitude, tuning into the child to understand his/her point of view, needs and interests.

Finally, many experiences that happened during the project were left out since it was impossible to recount so many moments of play, discovery and exploration. It was a great challenge to put into the written word situations that were of strong emotional significance to us. Despite that difficulty, we hope that our affection towards the children and the outdoors was transmitted, giving to this book a different format from other resources in this area. As a final message, we can only say:

● Go out with the children!
● Think outside the box!
● Step away from your comfort zone and dare to try!

There is a world of marvellous opportunities to discover that will not enter the classroom. Give yourself the opportunity to enjoy the outdoors with children and face the exciting challenge of creating memorable childhoods connected to the natural world.

Bibliography

Abbott-Chapman, J., Martin, K., Ollington, N., Venn, A., Dwyer, T. & Gall, S. (2014). The longitudinal association of childhood school engagement with adult educational and occupational achievement: Findings from an Australian national study. *British Educational Research Journal*, 40(1), 102–120. doi: 10.1002/berj.3031.

Adams, J. (2002). *Risk*. Abingdon: Routledge.

Agnew, J. (2011). Space and place. In: J. Agnew & D. N. Livingstone (eds), *The Sage handbook of geographic knowledge* (pp. 316–330). London: Sage Publications Limited.

Apter, M. J. (2007). *Danger: Our quest for excitement*. Oxford: Oneworld.

Athey, C. (2007). *Extending thought in young children: A parent–teacher partnership* (2nd edn). London: Sage.

Ball, D. J. (2002). *Playgrounds: Risks, benefits and choices* (Vol. 426/2002). London: Health and Safety Executive (HSE).

Bilton, H. (2010). *Outdoor learning in the early years: Management and innovation*. Abingdon: Routledge.

Bilton, H. & Crook, A. (2016). *Exploring outdoors ages 3–11: A guide for schools*. Abingdon: Routledge.

Blatchford, P., Pellegrini, A. D. & Baines, E. (2016). *The child at school: Interactions with peers and teachers* (2nd edn). Abingdon: Routledge.

Blurton-Jones, N. (1967). An ethological study of some aspects of social behaviour of children in nursery school. In D. Morris (ed.), *Primate ethology* (pp. 347–368). London: Weidenfeld and Nicolson.

Boschma, S. (2013). Tune up your immune system in the garden. Available at: www.mnn.com/health/healthy-spaces/stories/tune-up-your-immune-system-in-the-garden. Accessed 14 February 2016.

Broadhead, P. & Burt, A. (2012). *Understanding young children's learning through play*. Abingdon: Routledge.

Bronfenbrenner, U. (1979). *The ecology of human development*. Cambridge, MA: Harvard University Press.

Carson, R. (2012). *Maravilhar-se. Reaproximar a criança da natureza*. Santa Maria da Feira: Campo Aberto – Associação de Defesa da Natureza.

Christensen, P. & Mikkelsen, M. (2008). Jumping off and being careful: Children's strategies of risk management in everyday life. *Sociology of Health & Illness*, 30(1), 1–19.

Department for Education (2004). What makes an effective pre-school? Available at: www.ioe.ac.uk. Accessed 16 January 2016.

Department for Education (2011). Why do some children succeed 'against the odds'? Evidence from the EPPSE project. Available at: www.ioe.ac.uk/EPPSE_Why_do_some_disadvantaged_children_succeed_against_the_odds_Research_Bite.pdf. Accessed 16 January 2016.

Figueiredo, A. (2015). Interação criança-espaço exterior em jardim de infância. Unpublished doctoral thesis, University of Aveiro, Department of Education, Aveiro.

Fjørtoft, I. (2004). Landscape as playscape: The effects of natural environments on children's play and motor development. *Children, Youth and Environments*, 14(2), 21–44.

Gallahue, D. L. & Ozmun, J. C. (2006). *Understanding motor development* (6th edn). New York: McGraw-Hill.

Gill, T. (2007). *No fear: Growing up in a risk averse society*. London: Calouste Gulbenkian Foundation.

Gill, T. (2010). *Sem medo. Crescer numa sociedade com aversão ao risco*. Cascais: Princípia.

Goodenow, C. & Grady, K. E. (1993). The relationship of school belonging and friends' values to academic motivation among urban adolescent students. *Journal of Experimental Education*, 62(1), 60–71.

Goswami, U. (2013). *The Wiley-Blackwell handbook of childhood cognitive development* (2nd edn). Chichester: John Wiley.

Green, J. & Hart, L. (1998). Children's view of accident risks and prevention: A qualitative study. *Injury Prevention*, 4, 14–21.

Health and Safety Executive (2016). Children's play and leisure: Promoting a balanced approach. Available at: www.hse.gov.uk/entertainment/childs-play-statement.htm. Accessed 19 February 2016.

Herrington, S. & Studtmann, K. (1998). Landscape interventions: New directions for the design of children's outdoor play environments. *Landscape and Urban Planning*, 42(2–4), 191–205.

Holland, P. (2003). *We do not play with guns here: War, weapon and superhero play in the early years*. Maidenhead: Open University Press.

Howard, J. (2010). Early years practitioners' perceptions of play: An exploration of theoretical understanding, planning and involvement, confidence and barriers to practice. *Educational & Child Psychology*, 27(4), 91–102.

Huggins, V. & Wickett, K. (2011). Crawling and toddling in the outdoors: Very young children's learning. In S. Waite (ed.), *Children learning outside the classroom* (pp. 20–34). London: Sage Publications Ltd.

IoE (2016). The Effective Pre-School, Primary & Secondary Education (EPPSE) project. Available at: www.ioe.ac.uk/research/153.html. Accessed 31 January 2016.

Johnson. C. & Eccles, R. (2005). Acute cooling of the feet and the onset of common cold symptoms. *Family Practice*, 22(6), 608–613. doi: 10.1093/fampra/cmi072.

Jones, P. (2009). *Rethinking childhood*. London: Continuum.

Komulainen, S. (2007). The ambiguity of the child's voice in social research. *Childhood: A Global Journal of Child Research*, 18(1), 11–28.

Laevers, F. (1994). *The Leuven involvement scale for young children LIS-YC*. Leuven: Centre for Experiential Education.

Laevers, F. (2003). Experiential education: Making care and education more effective through well-being and involvement. In F. Laevers and L. Heylen (eds) *Involvement of children and teacher style* (pp. 13–24). Studia Paedagogica 35. Leuven: Leuven University Press.

Laevers, F., Moons, J. & Declercq, B. (2012). *A process-oriented monitoring system for the early years [POMS]*. Leuven: CEGO Publishers.

Leggett, N. & Ford, M. (2014). A fine balance: Understanding the roles educators and children play as intentional teachers and intentional learners within the Early Years Learning Framework. *Australasian Journal of Early Childhood*, 38(4), 42–50.

Little, H. (2006). Children's risk-taking behaviour: Implications for early childhood policy and practice. *International Journal of Early Years Education*, 14(2), 141–154.

Little, H. & Eager, D. (2010). Risk, challenge and safety: Implications for play quality and playground design. *European Early Childhood Education Research Journal*, 18(4), 497–513.

Maslow, A. H. (1962). *Towards a psychology of being*. Princeton, NJ: D. Van Nostrand Company.

Maslow, A. H. (2013). *A theory of human motivation*. Floyd, VA: Wilder Publications.

Maynard, T., Waters, J. & Clement, J. (2013). Child-initiated learning, the outdoor environment and the 'underachieving' child. *Early Years*, 33(3), 212–225.

McMillan, M. (1930). *The nursery school*. London: Dent and Sons.

Mendes, A., Aelenei, D., Papeila, A. L., Carreiro-Martins, P., Aguiar, L., Pereira, C., … Teixeira, J. P. (2014). Environmental and ventilation assessment in Child Day Care Centers in Porto: The ENVIRH Project. *Journal of Toxicology and Environmental Health, Part A*, 77(14–16), 931–943. doi: 10.1080/15287394.2014.911134

Mendonça, R. (2015). *Atividades em áreas naturais*. São Paulo: Ecofuturo.

Mercer, N. (2008). Talk and the development of reasoning and understanding. *Human Development*, 51(1), 90–100.

Mercer, N. & Littleton, K. (2007). *Dialogue and the development of children's thinking: A sociocultural approach*. Abingdon: Routledge.

Mitchell, R. & Popham, F. (2008). Effect of exposure to natural environment on health inequalities: An observational population study. *The Lancet*, 372(9650), 1655–1660.

Nutbrown, C. (2011). *Threads of thinking: Schemas and young children's learning*. London: Sage.

Pellegrini, A. (2009). *The role of play in human development*. Oxford: Oxford University Press.

Pollard, A. (2008). *Reflective teaching*. London: Continuum.

Portugal, G. (2011). No âmbito da educação em creche – o primado das relações e a importância dos espaços. In Conselho Nacional de Educação, *Educação da criança dos 0 aos 3 anos* (pp. 47–60). Lisbon: CNE.

Portugal, G. & Laevers, F. (2010). *Avaliação em educação pré-escolar. Sistema de acompanhamento de crianças*. Porto: Porto Editora.

Portugal, G., Carvalho, C. & Bento, G. (n.d.). *A Rosa dos Ventos. Orientações Pedagógicas para o trabalho com crianças dos 0 aos 3 anos*. Lisboa: Ministério da Educação e Ciência/ Direção Geral de Educação e o Ministério da Solidariedade, Emprego e Segurança Social/Instituto de Segurança Social. Documento em fase prévia a apreciação pública.

Pramling-Samuelsson, I. & Pramling, N. (2011). Didactics in early childhood education: Reflections on the volume. In N. Pramling & I. Pramling-Samuelsson (eds), *Educational encounters: Nordic studies on early childhood didactics* (pp. 242–256). Dordrecht: Springer.

Rose, J. & Rogers, S. (2012). *The role of the adult in early years settings*. Maidenhead: Open University Press.

Royal Society for the Prevention of Accidents (2016). Why educate children and young people about safety and risk? Available at: www.rospa.com/school-college-safety/teaching-safety/why-safety-and-risk-education/. Accessed 19 February 2016.

Sandseter, E. (2007). Categorizing risky play: How can we identify risk-taking in children's play? *European Early Childhood Education Research Journal*, 15(2), 237–252.

Sandseter, E. (2009). Risky play and risk management in Norwegian preschools: A qualitative observational study. *Safety Science Monitor*, 13(1), 1–12.

Sandseter, E. (2010). Scaryfunny: A qualitative study of risky play among preschool children. Unpublished doctoral thesis, Norwegian University of Science and Technology, Trondheim.

Schon, D. (1987). *Educating the reflective practitioner*. San Francisco, CA: Jossey-Bass.

Siegel, D. J. (2012). *The developing mind: How relationships and the brain interact to shape who we are*. New York: The Guildford Press.

Siraj-Blatchford, I., Sylva, K., Muttock, S., Gildren, R. & Bell, D. (2002). *Researching effective pedagogy in the early years research report RR356*. London: Department for Education and Skills.

Smith, S. J. (1998). *Risk and our pedagogical relation to children: On the playground and beyond.* New York: State University of New York Press.

Stephenson, A. (2003). Physical risk-taking: Dangerous or endangered? *Early Years*, 23(1), 35–43.

Sylva, K., Melhuish, E. C., Sammons, P., Siraj-Blatchford, I. & Taggart, B. (2004). *The effective provision of pre-school education (EPPE) project: Technical Paper 12 – The final report: Effective pre-school education.* London: DfES / Institute of Education, University of London.

Tovey, H. (2007). *Playing outdoors: Spaces and places, risk and challenges.* Maidenhead: Open University Press / McGraw-Hill Education.

Tranter, P. J. & Malone, K. (2004). Geographies of environmental learning: An exploration of children's use of school grounds. *Children's Geographies*, 2(1), 131–155.

Trevarthen, C. & Delafield-Butt, J. (2015). The infants' creative vitality, in projects of self-discovery and shared meaning: How they anticipate school, and make it fruitful. In S. Robson & S. Flannery Quin, *The Routledge international handbook of young children's thinking and understanding* (pp. 3–18). Abingdon: Routledge.

United Nations Assembly (1989). *Conventions on the rights of the child.* Geneva: United Nations High Commissioner for Human Rights. Available at: www.ohchr.org/EN/ProfessionalInterest/Pages/CRC.aspx. Accessed 24 January 2016.

Vygotsky, L. (1978). *Mind in society: The development of higher psychological processes.* Cambridge, MA: Harvard University Press.

Waite, S. (ed.) (2011). *Children learning outside the classroom: From birth to eleven.* London: Sage.

Waller, T., Sandseter, E. B. H., Wyver, S., Ärlemalm Hagsér, E. & Maynard, T. (2010). The dynamics of early childhood spaces: Opportunities for outdoor play? *European Early Childhood Education Research Journal*, 18(4), 437–443. doi: 10.1080/1350293X.2010.525917.

Wells, G. (1987). *The meaning makers: Children learning language and using language to learn.* London: Hodder and Stoughton.

Whitebread, D., Basilio, M., Kuvalja, M. & Verma, M. (2012). *The importance of play: A report on the value of children's play with a series of policy recommendations.* Brussels, Belgium: Toys Industries for Europe.

Wilson, E. O. (1984). *Biophilia.* Cambridge, MA: Harvard University Press.

Wood, E. (2013). *Play, learning and the early childhood curriculum.* London: Sage.

Wood, E. & Bennett, N. (2000). Changing theories, changing practice: Exploring early childhood teachers' professional learning. *Teaching and Teacher Education*, 16, 635–647.

Woolley, H. & Lowe, A. (2013). Exploring the relationship between design approach and play value of outdoor play spaces. *Landscape Research*, 38(1), 53–74.

Index

Note: Page numbers in **bold** are for figures.

Abbott-Chapman, J. 81
accidents, dealing with 113–15
Adams, J.
adult–child ratios 3, 115, 143
adults: childhood experiences 8, 97; as companions 79–82, 89–93; concerns about role in outdoor environment 9; risk perception 59–63; role in risk management 75, 113–17; *see also* parents
Aelenei, D. 108
Agnew, J. 10
Aguiar, L. 108
animals: playing and learning about 82–3, 139; *see also* birds; minibeasts
ants 29–30
Apter, M.J. 59
Ärlemalm Hagsér, E. 59
Athey, C. 40
autonomy 7, 10, 104

Baines, E. 59
Ball, D. J. 59, 61, 63
Basilio, M. 108
BBC 99
behaviour 18; appropriate 138; being attentive to 104, 125; changing 10–11; and risk 74
Bell, D. 107
belonging, sense of 81–2, 88
Bennett, N. 9
Bento, G. 19, 80
Bilton, H. 6, 10, 40, 79, 100, 107
biophilia 21
birds 22–7; anatomy 24, 26, 59; dead 24; nests 22–3
Blatchford, P. 59
Blurton-Jones, N. 59
body awareness 7
Boschma, S. 43
brain development 11, 12

Broadhead, P. 94
Bronfenbrenner, U. 104
Burt, A. 94
butterflies 27–9

camping 90–1, 111
Carreiro-Martins, P. 108
Carson, R. 19, 145
Carvalho, C. 19, 80
Centro Social Infantil de Aguada de Baixo (CENSI) 1, 3; adult–child ratios 3; daily routine 3, 5; parental support and participation 5, 8; project background 6–7
challenges *see* climbing challenges; physical challenges
change: in children's behaviour 10–11; reflection and evaluation as a means to 9–10
chasing games 71
child development 8, 11–13, 96, 100, 103, 108, 145; cognitive aspects of ix, 62, 108, 123; emotional aspects of 62, 104–5, 108, 123; physical aspects of 62, 108, 123; and risky play 58, 59, 61, 63, 113; and rough and tumble play 71, 74, 75; social aspects of 77–8, 81, 104, 104–5, 108, 123
Christensen, P. 74
Clement, J. 6, 43
climbing challenges x, 62; hills **65**, 65–8, **66**, **67**; tree houses 63–5; trees 33, 61
clothes 100, 105, 108, 135, 143; changing 7; dirty 8; waterproof 8, **106**
cognitive development ix, 62, 108, 123
colours 33
comfort in outdoor areas 135; *see also* clothes
community visits 114, 142–4
companionship 76–94
concentration 21, 55, 57, 93, 100, 105
conflict 94
connectedness, sense of 81–2

contemplation, importance of 38
conversations 41; group 87–8
cooperation x, 7, 10, 43, 45–6, 56, 77–8, 81, 94
creativity 55, 93, 105
critical thinking 9
Crook, A. 10, 100
curiosity 19

danger 19, 24, 46–7, 59, 62, 63, 74, 75, 105, 108, 113–14; parents fears about 8; risk distinguished from 59
death 24
Declercq, B. 104–5
Delafield-Butt, J.
Department for Education 113
development *see* child development; emotional development; physical development; professional development; social development; sustainable development
discovery: bird's nest 22, 23; of dead animals 24; power of 19; resources for 125–8, **126**, **127**, **128**, **130**, **131**; sharing 30, **82**; unexpected moments of **98**, **99**
disease 108
Dwyer, T. 81

Eager, D. 58
Eccles, R. 108
Effective Provision of Preschool Education (EPPE) 104, 107
Einstein, A. xi
emotional development 62, 104–5, 108, 123
emotions 19, 29, 71, 115
empathy x, 24, 76, 78, 82, 146
enabling environments, creating 78
'Enchanted Moorish' legend 89–90
energy 55, 93, 100, 105
entrepreneurship 62
Environment and Health in children day care centres (ENVIRH) 108
EPPE *see* Effective Provision of Preschool Education
equipment 75, 96, 105, **106**, 121; *see also* fixed structures; resources for outdoor learning
evaluation: as means to change 9–10; project 116
experiential attitude 104

Experiential Education approach 100
experimenting 40, 41
exploration 19, 39; creating the right environment for 132, 135; opportunities in the community for 142, 143; resources for 125–8, **126**, **127**, **128**, **130**, **131**

facilitator role of teacher 100, 103, 104
falling from heights 68, 69
families: playing at 86–7; *see also* parents
farm produce 36
farm visits 13, **17**, 36–7, 68, 70, 90–1
fascination 55, 105
fear: adults' 69; learning to deal with 61
fighting games 71
Figueiredo, A. 6
fixed structures **133**, **135**; construction of 132, **134**; for socialisation and physical challenges 132; *see also* ramps; tree houses
Fjørtoft, I. 39
flowers **18**, 28, **30**
foods, tasting new 36, 38
Ford, M. 6
freedom of choice 100, 102, 123
friendship 81, 87
fruit and vegetables 36–7

Gall, S. 81
Gallahue, D. L. 20
gardening 36–8
gene expression 11
Gildren, R. 107
Gill, T. 61, 62, 108
Goodenow, C. 81
Goswami, U. 42
Grady, K. E. 81
Green, J. 74
group conversations 87–8
growing plants 36–8
guess who is… game 88
guns and swords, sticks as 71

happiness 21
Hart, L. 74
health x, 21, 43, 105–6, 108
Health and Safety Executive (HSE) 62
healthy eating habits 36, 37
Herrington, S. 39
hills, going up and down **65**, 65–8, **66**, **67**

Holland, P. 59
Howard, J. 6
Huggins, V. 21

inclusion 123
indoor environment, relationship with outdoors 138–41
interaction 104–5; adult–child 3, **4**, 7, 8, 79–80, 100, 104, **117**; between children 30, **31**, 43, **65**, 81, **86**, 87, 94; with natural world 33, 43; with risk 61, 62

involvement: attributes of 55, 93; of children 6, 9, 10, 26, 46, 49, 55, 93–4, 100, 104, 105, 124, 132; of parents/families 8, 108–13, 132, 135; and teacher as learning facilitator 103

Johnson, C. 108
Jones, P. 12
joy 19–21, 88

Komulainen, S. 12
Kuvalja, M. 108

Laevers, F. 6, 55, 93, 104–5
language development x, 41, 42, 113
learning facilitator role 100, 103, 104
leaves 48
Leggett, N. 6
literacy 54
Little, H. 58
Littleton, K. 41
logistics 7, 8, 10
love 21, 81, 86
Lowe, A. 39

McMillan, M. ix, 19
Malone, K. 39
Martin, K. 81
Maslow, A. H. 81, 104
materials 10, 13, 78, 120, 124; construction 132; introducing new 103, 104; quality and quantity of 128; storage of 122, 132, 135, **136**; use in different ways 128; *see also* equipment; natural materials; resources for outdoor learning
Maynard, T. 6, 43, 59
Melhuish, E. C. 104
Mendes, A. 108
Mendonça, R. 80

Mercer, N. 41
mess: dealing with 9, 132, 135; *see also* mud
Mikkelsen, M. 74
mind, functioning of 11–12
minibeasts 29–32, 54, 139
Mitchell, R. 21
monitoring activities 10, 116, 118
Moons, J. 104–5
motivation 62, 81, 105; intrinsic 105
mud 13, 21, **33**, 49, **50**, 57, 84, 121, 122; painting with 51, **52**
mums and dads: playing at 86–7; *see also* parents
museum of outdoor play 139, **140**
mushrooms 46–7
Muttock, S. 107
myths about under threes 38, 57, 74–5, 93–4

natural materials 39, 40, **53**, 122; *see also* mud; sand; soil; sticks
natural world: as all encompassing learning place ix; colours of 33; developing affection and connection towards 21; discovering and experiencing 18–38; play in 39–57; rhythms of 21
Nature wildlife website 100
needs, basic 104, 105
Nutbrown, C. 40

Ollington, N. 81
oral language x, 41, 42
outdoors: relationship with indoor environment 138–41; role of adults 9; unique opportunities offered by 122
overstimulation, negative consequences of 38
Ozmun, J.C. 20

painting 51–3, **52**, **53**, **54**
parents: interaction with children 8; construction of fixed structures 132; involvement/support 5, 8, 90–1, 108–13, 132, 135; own childhood experiences 8; points to note when considering 112; reassuring 8, 113–14; relationships with 91, 108–13
pedagogical framing 107
pedagogical relationship 102

Pellegrini, A. D. 6, 59
Pereira, C. 108
persistence 55, 62, 93, 100, 105
personality 11, 81
photographs 10, 139
physical challenges: fixed structures for 132; *see also* climbing challenges
physical development 62, 108, 123
physiological needs 104
planning the outdoor space: changing/introducing new structures or objects 121; comfort concerns 135; dynamics of the environment 120–2; fixed structures 132; inclusion 123; participation in 123–4; storage systems 122, 132, 135, **136**; sustainability 122; time issues in 124–5; *see also* resources for outdoor learning
plants: collecting 54–7; growing and harvesting 36–8
play: as letting off steam 6; right to 6
Pollard, A. 59
Popham, F. 21
Portugal: climate 6; early childhood education 6, 100; Environment and Health in children day care centres (ENVIRH) 108
Portugal, G. 6, 19, 80, 93, 104
Pramling, N. 9
Pramling-Samuelson, I. 9
preparing to go outside and return 7
problem-solving 61, 62, 76, 81
professional development 6–10, 98, 124

quality, educational 104, 107
questions 41, 42

rain 32
ramps 68
record keeping 10, 116, 118
reflection 104; critical 118–19; as means to change 9–10
relationships 12, 104; with parents/families 91, 108–13; pedagogical 102; *see also* companionship; friendship; interaction
repetition, as important learning strategy 40–1, 44, 68
resources for outdoor learning 125–8, **126**, **127**, **128**, **130**, **131**; accessibility of 128; list of different types provided 130; open-ended 128, **129**, 141; portability

of 128; quantity and quality 128; storage systems 122, 132, 135, **136**; transportation of 135, **136**; use in different ways 128; *see also* equipment; materials
rickets 108
rights of children 6, 12
risk x, 42, 46, 58–75, **69**, 108; adults' perception of 59–63; adults' role in managing 75, 113–16; children's ability to evaluate 74; danger distinguished from 59; defining 58–9; as interactive phenomenon 61; out of adult's sight 68–71; role in child development 58, 59, 61, 63, 113; when it's not worth taking 73–4
Rogers, S. 6, 63, 118
role play: playing at mums and dads 86–7; rough and tumble 71
Rose, J. 6, 63, 118
rough and tumble play x, 59, 71
routines, importance of 87
Royal Society for the Prevention of Accidents (RoSPA) 58, 62, 77

safety 46, 47, 108, 116, 143; *see also* risk
safety needs 104
Sammons, P. 104
sand 121
Sandseter, E. B. H. 59, 61, 74, 75
schemas 40, 44, 68
Schon, D. 118
scissors, using 54–6
seasons 33
self-esteem 42, 48, 81
self-regulation 7, 38
sensitivity 104
sensory experiences 19–21
shared experiences 76–94
shared understanding 79–80
sharing x, 10, 12, 43, 76, 102
shyness 11
Siegel, D. J. 11, 12, 104
silence, importance of 38
Siraj-Blatchford, I. 104, 107
sleepovers 91
smells 37, 38
Smith, S.J. 59, 74
snails 30–2
social development 77–8, 81, 104, 105, 108, 123

soil 43, 49–54, **111;** *see also* mud
Stephenson, A. 10, 59, 62, 63, 75
sticks 40, 44, **71**; play fighting with 71, **72**
stimulation 104; over- 38
storage systems 122, 132, 135, **136**
strength 42
stress 11–12; reduction of 21
Studtmann, K. 39
sun 32, 33
sustainable development 21
swords and guns, sticks as 71
Sylva, K. 104, 107

Taggart, B. 104
team meetings 9–10
terrible twos 11
Teixeira, J. P. 108
thunder storms 32
time 7, 57, 124; and planning the outdoor
    space 124
touching 40
Tovey, H. 10, 19, 21, 41, 42, 75
transport of resources 135, **136**
Tranter, P. J. 39
tree houses 63–5
trees, climbing 33, 61
Trevarthen, C.
trust 82, 102

understanding 41; shared 79–80

unexpected, the: play with 46–54;
    practising 62
United Nations Convention on the
    Rights of the Child 6, 12

Venn, A. 81
Verma, M. 108
video recording 10
Vygotsky, L. 93, 104, 105

Waite, S. 62
Waller, T. 59
water ix, 20, 32, 49–54, 84–5, 122;
    resources to use with 125, 127
Waters, J. 6, 43
weapons, sticks as 44, 71, **72**
weather 7, 32–3, 46, 48; impact on
    outdoor space 121
well-being 21, 104, 105–6
Wells, G. 19
Whitebread, D. 108
Wickett, K. 21
Wilson, E. O. 21
Wood, E. 6, 9
Woodland Trust 99
Woolley, H. 39
written records 10, 116
Wyver, S. 59

Zone of Proximal Development 93, 105